Academic Foundations in English

Building a Career in Science

Level 1

Michael Schulman
Hiroyo Yoshida

Australia · Brazil · Mexico · Singapore · United Kingdom · United States

Academic Foundations in English: Building a Career in Science, Level 1

Michael Schulman / Hiroyo Yoshida

© 2019 Cengage Learning K.K.

ALL RIGHTS RESERVED. No part of this work covered by the copyright herein may be reproduced, transmitted, stored, or used in any form or by any means—graphic, electronic, or mechanical, including but not limited to photocopying, recording, scanning, digitizing, taping, Web distribution, information networks, or information storage and retrieval systems—without the prior written permission of the publisher.

"National Geographic", "National Geographic Society" and the Yellow Border Design are registered trademarks of the National Geographic Society ® Marcas Registradas

Photo Credits:
front cover: © RICHARD NOWITZ/National Geographic Creative; p. 9: © olaser/iStock.com; p. 22(t), 34(t), 40, 46(t), 52(t), 62(t), 68: © Ductru/iStock.com; p. 22(b), 23, 28(all), 29, 34(m), 35, 41(all), 46(b), 47, 52(b), 53, 62(b), 63, 69(all), 75, 81, 87: © rizal999/iStock.com; p. 31: © Michael Schulman; p. 34: (b) © daboost/iStock.com; p. 54: © Adobest/iStock.com; p. 55: (t) © johnwoodcock/iStock.com, (b) © Alamy (RM)/Pacific Press Service; p. 70: © Michael Schulman; p. 71: © Michael Schulman; p. 76: (l) © https://www.nasa.gov/topics/earth/features/japanquake/japan-20110405.html,
(r) © PeteDraper/iStock.com; p. 82: © http://chandra.harvard.edu/resources/illustrations/milkyWay.html;
p. 83: (t) © https://commons.wikimedia.org/wiki/File:5_Local_Galactic_Group_(ELitU).png,
(b) © https://commons.wikimedia.org/wiki/File:6_Virgo_Supercluster_(ELitU).png

For permission to use material from this textbook or product, e-mail to **eltjapan@cengage.com**

ISBN: 978-4-86312-353-3

National Geographic Learning | Cengage Learning K.K.
No. 2 Funato Building 5th Floor
1-11-11 Kudankita, Chiyoda-ku
Tokyo 102-0073
Japan

Tel: 03-3511-4392
Fax: 03-3511-4391

ON THE COVER

The Ray and Maria Stata Center for Computer Information Service at the Massachusetts Institute of Technology in Massachusetts, USA.

学習者のみなさんへ

*Academic Foundations in English: Building a Career in Science, Level 1*は、英語を外国語として学習する理工系学生のための総合英語学習演習教材です。理系の大学生の会話から展開する各ユニットは、アカデミック・ライティングに不可欠なパラフレーズと要約に主眼を置き、それらの技能を効果的に習得できる演習で構成されています。これらの演習は同時に、TOEFLやTOEICなどのテストで必要なスキルの向上も目的としています。

各ユニットの**Dialog**では、日本の東京太平洋大学理工学部の学生たちと寺田教授、ニューヨークのハッブル大学からやって来たブラウン教授、留学生のビクターとセリーナ、彼らのキャンパスでの交流が会話として描かれます。これに先立つ**Quick Survey**では、**Dialog**のトピックに関連した5つの質問が提示され、アンケートを行います。クラスメートたちと自分の意見を比較してみましょう。

Dialogに続く**Exercises**は3つのパートで構成されています。**Part 1**と**2**では**Dialog**（Unit 12～14では**Lecture**）を要約した英文の音声を聞き取る演習（**Dictation**）を行います。**Part 3**では**Dialog**の内容把握問題に答えて理解度を確認後、自分で**Dialog**の要約文を書きます。その際、**Part 1**と**2**の要約文の中で内容が同じでもパラフレーズされている（表現方法が異なっている）箇所にも注目してみましょう。これらの演習は、英語で要約パラグラフを書く練習として役立つだけでなく、TOEFLやTOEICに対応するリスニング能力やTOEFL iBTのスピーキングやライティングのスキル向上にも役立ちます。さらに、これに続く**Grammar Focus**でも、TOEFL ITPやTOEICに頻出される文法問題の演習を行います。

最後の**Writing Assignments**では、英文を書く演習を行います。**Making a Career Plan**はキャリア教育のエクササイズです。これまでの振り返り（自分史の作成）と自己分析を英語で行ったり、現状の自分を理解するために現在の自分の英文履歴書を書いたり、就職活動時の自分を想定した「なるべき自分」についての「未来の英文履歴書」を作成したりします。**Writing a Paragraph**では、クラスメートとブレーンストーミングした（アイデアを十分出し合った）後で、様々なパターンに合わせて英文パラグラフを書く演習を行います。**Dialog**の演習で学習したパラフレーズを実践しながら、まずは一つでも多くの英文を書くことに挑戦してみましょう。

著　者

Table of Contents

学習者のみなさんへ ………………………………………… 3
Characters ……………………………………………………… 6
音声ファイルの利用方法 …………………………………… 7

Unit	Title	Grammar Focus
Unit 1	Human Library and Profile	Rephrasing with Prepositions, Adverbs, and Conjunctions
Unit 2	Keeping a Career Log	Verb Forms (1)
Unit 3	Rules in the School Library	Time and Place, Inversion
Unit 4	Amazing Inventions	Verbs Related to Perception
Unit 5	The Sun Is White	Adjectives and Adjective Clauses
Unit 6	Online Social Networking	Nouns and Noun Clauses
Unit 7	Robotic Cleaner	Nouns—Countable / Uncountable
Unit 8	Water Survey	Verb Forms (2)
Unit 9	Optical Illusions	Comparative and Superlative Adjectives
Unit 10	School Planning and Design	Verb Forms (3) and If-Clauses
Unit 11	Art and Science	Adjective Clauses—Relative Clauses
Unit 12	The Structure of the Universe (1)	
Unit 13	The Structure of the Universe (2)	
Unit 14	The Structure of the Universe (3)	

Example of a Future Resume 92
Glossary 94
Writing Assignment Submission Form 99

Writing Assignments: Making a Career Plan / Writing a Paragraph	Page
Making a Career Plan (1): Writing strengths and weaknesses, personal history / Writing a curriculum vitae	8
Making a Career Plan (2): Set a provisional goal with an occupation and necessary qualifications / Writing about future goals in chronological order / Writing a curriculum vitae representing the future	14
Writing a Spatial Order Paragraph: Organizing the layout of a room	20
Writing a Descriptive Paragraph (1): With adjectives describing positive factors / Describing an admirable person	26
Writing a Descriptive Paragraph (2): With plural adjectives describing a device / Describing a favorite possession	32
Writing a Sequential Order Paragraph: Discussing a first experience	38
Writing a Definitive Paragraph: Discussing an ideal robot	44
Writing a Process Analysis Paragraph: Discussing an interesting experiment	50
Writing a Comparison or Contrast Paragraph: Comparing your belongings to others	56
Writing a Persuasive Paragraph: Expressing an opinion about a building, with reasons	62
Writing an Argumentative Paragraph: Discussing agreement or disagreement with a statement, with reasons	68
Writing a Summary Paragraph (1): Summarizing a lecture	74
Writing a Summary Paragraph (2): Summarizing a lecture	80
Writing a Summary Paragraph (3): Summarizing a lecture	86

Characters

Professor Brown (Anthony Brown)

He is a professor at Hubble University in New York. He has been staying in Japan as a visiting professor, while conducting research on environmental science and education. He likes astronomy and architecture.

Victor

He is a second-year student at Hubble University. He has been staying in Japan as an exchange student. His major is Electrical, Electronic and Communications Engineering and he really likes technology.

Serena

She is also a sophomore at Hubble University. She has been staying in Japan as an exchange student. Her major is Architecture, and as a child she won many awards for her watercolor paintings. She is brilliant and a good inventor.

Professor Terada

He is a professor at Tokyo Pacific University. He is also doing research on environmental science and education. He likes architecture, so he is good friends with Professor Brown.

Kimi

She is a first-year student at Tokyo Pacific University. Her major is Civil and Environmental Engineering. She is a thoughtful and diligent person. She wants to help people, and work as a civil servant in the future.

Ryoma

He is a freshman at Tokyo Pacific University. His major is Biomedical Engineering. He won the first prize in a major speech contest at his university in 2017. He will be an exchange student and has studied at Hubble University.

Taro

He is a sophomore at Tokyo Pacific University. His major is Mechanical Engineering. He grew up in Ohio, USA and attended elementary school there. He wants to be a computer game creator.

Ari

She is a junior at Tokyo Pacific University. Her major is Chemistry. She likes traveling abroad and has visited many cities including London, New York, Los Angeles, Hanoi, and Manila. She is an inspiration to her classmates.

Shun

He is a senior at Tokyo Pacific University. His major is Architecture and he has decided to go to graduate school. He is a modest boy, but has a quick mind. He is talented at graphic design. He was an exchange student at Hubble University.

音声ファイルの利用方法

🎧 00 のアイコンがある箇所の音声ファイルにアクセスできます。

https://ngljapan.com/afie-1-audio/

❶ 上記 URL にアクセス、または QR コードをスマートフォンなどのリーダーでスキャン
❷ 表示されるファイル名をクリックして音声ファイルをダウンロードまたは再生

Unit 1
Human Library and Profile

Quick Survey Ask the following five questions to your partner. Then, write your answers, your partner's answers, and the most popular answers in your group or class.

Question	Your answer	Your partner's answer	Most popular answer
1. Have you ever thought about your future?			
2. What do you remember most from your elementary school days?			
3. What kind of class did you like most in junior high school or high school?			
4. What are some of the most impressive events of your life so far?			
5. What are you good at or what makes you feel good?			

Dialog 02

> A group of university students are joining an event called "Human Library" in the school library. During this event, the audience can choose a person and listen to his or her story. Professor Brown is one of the "Human Books" in the event and he has composed his presentation based on his personal experience before he became a university professor.

Prof. Brown: Thanks for listening. Do you have any questions? *(One of the students is raising his hand.)* Yes, you. Can I have your name?

Ryoma: I'm Ryoma. I'm very interested in your background, especially how you became a professor. I probably won't become a professor, but I got more serious about my future after learning your story. I would like to be an engineer doing work related to development of medical devices. How can I begin if I want to achieve this objective?

Prof. Brown: It's a tough question, but I'll try to help you. The most important thing is to start to learn about yourself and listen to your voice inside.

10 **Ryoma:**	Learn about myself and listen to my voice? I'm not sure how to do it.	
Prof. Brown:	Well, I mean that you must know who you are, what makes you happy, and what you need to do to attain your goal.	
Ryoma:	I still don't get it. Can you elaborate?	
Prof. Brown:	Sure. First of all, it may be a good idea to write your personal history, like the story I told you about myself a few minutes ago.	
Ryoma:	I see. So, should I write about the schools I've attended and any experience I have?	
Prof. Brown:	You bet! Then, you can make a list of your strengths and weaknesses.	
20 **Ryoma:**	Now I understand. I should write about what I'm good at, what I like, and vice versa, and this can help me to look back through my past experiences. As a result, I can learn about myself in a new, objective way. Am I right?	
25 **Prof. Brown:**	That's right!	
Ryoma:	So, do you mean I need to profile myself?	
Prof. Brown:	I think you've got it.	

Exercises   Dialog Summary

Part 1 [Dictation] 🎧 03

Listen and fill in the blanks.

After the Human Library event, Professor Brown and the (　　　) have a discussion. One of the students, Ryoma, asks the professor a (　　　) question about how to attain his goal to become an engineer (　　　) (　　　) development of medical devices. Professor Brown (　　　) that he should start to learn about (　　　) and listen to (　　　) voice inside: who he is, what makes him happy, and what he needs to do to (　　　) his goal.

Part 2 [Dictation] 🎧 04

Listen and fill in the blanks.

Professor Brown offers Ryoma a (　　　) way to write his personal history in order to attain his (　　　). Ryoma understands that he should write about all of his past schools and experiences, and make a list of his strengths and weaknesses. He also understands that these activities (　　　) him (　　　) back through his past experiences to help see himself from the (　　　) in a new way. In (　　　) (　　　), he needs to (　　　) himself using this (　　　).

Part 3 [Writing a summary]

Answer the following questions and then write a summary of the dialog.

1. What does Ryoma ask Professor Brown?

   _____

2. What is a personal history?

   _____

3. Why does Professor Brown suggest writing a personal history?

   _____

Grammar Focus: Rephrasing with Prepositions, Adverbs, and Conjunctions

Unit 1

Rephrasing can change the structure of a sentence. One way to do this is to focus on the prepositions, adverbs, and conjunctions that are related to connecting parts of sentences, phrases or clauses.

Fill in the blanks so that both the first and second sentences in each question have a similar meaning.

1. My sister went to England just a day after she came back from the academic conference in Kyushu.
   ⇨ Just a day after (　　　　　) from the academic conference in Kyushu, my sister went to England.

2. Before you pour the liquid, please make sure you are using the right beaker.
   ⇨ Please make sure you are using the right beaker before (　　　　　) the liquid.

3. All objects regardless of their masses accelerate at the same rate because gravity exists.
   ⇨ All objects with different masses accelerate at the same rate due (　　　　　) gravity.

4. All students are required to wear a lab coat while the experiment is running.
   ⇨ All students have to put on a lab coat (　　　　　) the experiment.

5. Although most of his experiments failed, Edison learned a lot from them.
   ⇨ (　　　　　) the failure of most of his experiments, Edison learned a lot from them.

6. These yellow blooms resemble butterflies when they are open.
   ⇨ These yellow blooms resemble butterflies when (　　　　　).

7. The telescope is positioned above the mount, and in the (　　　　　) of the enclosure.
   ⇨ The mount is positioned (　　　　　) the telescope, which is surrounded by the enclosure.

8. My concentration (　　　　　) my calculations was interrupted by the noise from the neighboring construction site yesterday.
   ⇨ The noise from the adjacent construction site prevented me from (　　　　　) on (　　　　　) calculations yesterday.

9. As students were not sure about which chemical to use when cleaning the machine, one of them contacted the manufacturer by phone.
   ⇨ Students were uncertain as to which chemical to use when cleaning the machine, (　　　　　) one of them called the manufacturer.

10. The exhibit outside the observatory was cancelled because of the heavy rain.
    ⇨ The heavy rain resulted (　　　　　) the cancellation of the exhibit outside the observatory.

Writing Assignments — Making a Career Plan (1)

A Write a list of your strengths and weaknesses in English. Then, discuss it with your partner.

Strengths	Weaknesses

B Write about your personal history in English. Include details, following the steps below.

1) Start by writing basic facts about yourself.

2) Briefly write about notable achievements, including anything particularly interesting or unusual.

3) Write about hardships you have overcome, including anything particularly interesting or unusual.

4) Finally, add your skills and qualifications.

C Fill in the blanks to help you write your curriculum vitae in English. Include the details you wrote in **B** above. You can refer to the sample on page 92.

Family name	
First name	
Middle name (if any)	
Place of birth	
Present address	
Permanent address	
Special notes such as notable achievements or hardships you have overcome	
Skills	
Qualifications	

Unit 2 Keeping a Career Log

Quick Survey

Ask the following five questions to your partner. Then, write your answers, your partner's answers, and the most popular answers in your group or class.

Question	Your answer	Your partner's answer	Most popular answer
1. What type of job most interests you?			
2. Have you ever kept a diary or journal?			
3. Would you prefer to use a phone or notebook for a journal?			
4. Do you have any daily routines?			
5. Are you a person who tries to complete your plans?			

Dialog 05

The students are still asking questions to Professor Brown, who is acting as a book for the Human Library event.

Kimi: I'm a civil engineering student, but unlike Ryoma, I don't know what I'd like to do in the future. I understand that I should profile myself in the way you advised us. What should we do next?

Prof. Brown: After you learn about who you really are, you can set your provisional goal. It's just practice, so you can change it whenever you'd like.

Kimi: OK. So I'm going to have to do something to set my goal, right? So, I'll investigate and consider different fields, and choose one of them. Sounds good?

Prof. Brown: Yeah. After that, you can focus on what you need to do. You should find out what kinds of skills you need to accomplish your career goal.

Kimi: In what way?

Prof. Brown: Once you set your goal, you can outline your future goal and plan the things you should do for it in the long term. This is important to help develop your skills and make use of your talent.

Kimi: I see. How do I do that?

Prof. Brown: I suggest keeping a career log.

Kimi: What's that?

Prof. Brown: It's a type of journal. Every day, you should record everything that you do, using your phone or notebook. It may be a good idea to write more comprehensively about some important matters or information later.

Kimi: That makes sense. So it's probably best to summarize my journal weekly, and then monthly. Is that what you're saying?

Prof. Brown: Exactly. In addition, you should review your journal at the end of each semester. It helps you to understand what you need to do to prepare and then take action to help achieve your future goal. In this way, you can easily remember what you have done and what you haven't done.

Kimi: Sounds like a plan. It will be a record of my difficult days before the job hunting process starts.

Exercises Dialog Summary

Part 1 Dictation 🎧 06

Listen and fill in the blanks.

　During the discussion after the Human Library event, Kimi asks a question. She doesn't know what to do next for her future after (　　　　　) herself. The professor advises her to set a (　　　　　) (　　　　　) and says she should focus on what kinds of skills she needs to (　　　　　) her career goal.

Part 2 Dictation 🎧 07

Listen and fill in the blanks.

　During the discussion with Professor Brown, Kimi asks a question about what to do next for her future after profiling herself. The professor advises her to set a (　　　　　) goal and says she should find out (　　　　　) she needs to do to accomplish her career goal. Professor Brown also suggests (　　　　　) (　　　　　) (　　　　　) a career log and says that it helps to outline (　　　　　) things and plan for a future goal in the long term. Although it's a (　　　　　) record, the best way is to (　　　　　) the journal weekly and monthly, and finally review them at the end of each semester.

Part 3 Writing a summary

Answer the following questions and then write a summary of the dialog.

1. What is Kimi's question?

　_____

2. What does the professor advise her to do?

　_____

3. What is a career log? Why is it necessary?

　_____

Grammar Focus: Verb Forms (1)

When we use more than one verb in a sentence, we need to use a variety of forms. Different verbs can take different forms. Some verbs may be followed by gerunds, but others can be followed by infinitives.

Change each of the underlined parts if necessary.

1. The main task of a teaching assistant is to help students safely <u>do</u> an experiment in a laboratory. → _____

2. The leader of a group suggests <u>try</u> different methods to improve the process. → _____

3. A web search engine is designed to let you <u>search</u> for information on the internet. → _____

4. The professor reminded students <u>send</u> her a report as an attachment by e-mail. → _____

5. All the architectural students will spend much of their time <u>get</u> their assignments done next week. → _____

6. Although safety equipment can be heavy, most people don't mind <u>wear</u> it in a laboratory. → _____

7. Swimming allows you <u>do</u> full-body exercise, and to work your body without harsh impact to your skeletal system. → _____

8. We'll never forget <u>watch</u> the solar eclipse over the Canadian mountains five years ago. → _____

9. Remember <u>remove</u> the chemical from the skin immediately in order to minimize injury due to chemical burns. → _____

10. Some companies intend <u>establish</u> an ethics committee on artificial intelligence. → _____

Unit 2

Writing Assignments — Making a Career Plan (2)

A Set your provisional goal three years ahead, during your search for a job. Choose an occupation you would like to have in the future. Then, think about what kinds of qualifications you need for this job and list them in English.

[Example]
The occupation I chose is: math teacher
The things I need to do are:
- Work hard to receive appropriate credits for classes
- Teaching practice
- Get the 1st level (1st-Kyu) on the Sugaku Kentei Certificate (a test for measuring practical skills in mathematics)

The occupation I chose is:
The things I need to do are:

B Write about your future goals in English, including the major activities and experiences you need to achieve them, in chronological order. They may be related to the list you made in **A** above.

C Write your future curriculum vitae in English to fit your job hunting activities in a few years. Include the details you wrote in **B** above. You can refer to the sample on page 92.

Unit 3
Rules in the School Library

Quick Survey Ask the following five questions to your partner. Then, write your answers, your partner's answers, and the most popular answers in your group or class.

Question	Your answer	Your partner's answer	Most popular answer
1. Where do you usually do your homework?			
2. How often do you use the school library?			
3. Would you like to study alone in the library, or would you rather study with your friends?			
4. Do you like to read books? What kind of books do you like?			
5. Do you like to watch DVDs? What kind of DVDs do you like to watch?			

Dialog 08

> Professor Brown becomes interested in the library that he used during a recent human library event. There are a lot of fascinating books and materials there, and he's decided to borrow a copy of a magazine and a DVD for his class.

Librarian:	Good morning.
Prof. Brown:	Good morning. I'm Anthony Brown, a professor at Hubble University, and I'm going to teach here this semester.
Librarian:	Nice to meet you, Professor Brown. May I help you?
5 **Prof. Brown:**	I'd like to borrow a copy of *Time* magazine and a DVD.
Librarian:	I'm sorry, but you can't take out DVDs from the library. They must be viewed inside the library.
Prof. Brown:	OK. Well, I'd like to check if this DVD is appropriate for my students. If it's all

	right, I'll recommend it. Where is the audiovisual corner?
10 Librarian:	It's on the right, next to the windows.
Prof. Brown:	I see. I'll do that during the lunch hour. I also need to check if Chemical Abstracts is available. How can students get access to it?
Librarian:	They can use the databases on the website. The computers are on the left side.
Prof. Brown:	All right. By the way, when should I return this magazine?
15 Librarian:	You can borrow it for a week, so you should return it by Friday.
Prof. Brown:	OK, thank you.
Librarian:	We have a security system at the main entrance. It helps us to safeguard the books by preventing the unauthorized removal of material. So, you need to check out the book with your ID card before you go.
20 Prof. Brown:	I see. May I check it out now?
Librarian:	Of course, you can do it here at this counter. Can I have your ID card?
Prof. Brown:	Here you are.
Librarian:	Thank you. *(The librarian hands Prof. Brown the book and the ID card.)* Here you go. Next time, you can use the self-checkout machine near the stairs in the back.
25 Prof. Brown:	All right. No problem. Thank you very much.
Librarian:	You're welcome.

Exercises Dialog Summary

Part 1 Dictation 🎧 09

Listen and fill in the blanks.

Professor Brown wants to (　　　　) a copy of *Time* magazine and a DVD. The librarian tells him that it is not (　　　　) to take DVDs (　　　　) (　　　　) the library and they must be viewed (　　　　) the library. So, the professor only (　　　　) (　　　　) the magazine.

Part 2 Dictation 🎧 10

Listen and fill in the blanks.

Professor Brown would like to take out a copy of *Time* magazine and a DVD, but the librarian tells him that people are only (　　　　) to view DVDs inside the library. The professor needs to check the DVD, so he tells the librarian that he will do it during the lunch (　　　　). The professor also confirms that his students are able to use the databases of Chemical Abstracts (　　　　) (　　　　) (　　　　). Finally, he checks out the magazine, and the librarian tells him to return it (　　　　) (　　　　). The librarian tells the professor that he needs to check out the book (　　　　) (　　　　) (　　　　) (　　　　) because of the security systems (　　　　) (　　　　) (　　　　), and next time he can use the (　　　　) (　　　　) (　　　　) the stairs (　　　　) the back.

Part 3 Writing a summary

Answer the following questions and then write a summary of the dialog.

1. What does Professor Brown want to do and what does he finally check out?

   _____

2. When does the magazine need to be returned?

   _____

3. Where is the self-checkout machine, and what is it?

   _____

Grammar Focus: Time and Place, Inversion

We use phrases with prepositions and adverbs when we describe time and place. They are usually placed at the end of a clause or sentence. However, some emphatic expressions should be placed at the beginning of a clause or sentence and need to have an unusual structure, called inversion.

Choose a phrase from the box below to complete each of the following sentences. Use a capital letter to begin the first word of each sentence.

1. The blueprints for the new building are on hold (   ).
2. A radical change in the formula for a new drug will take place (   ).
3. The scientific program has aired continuously (   ).
4. (   ) did scientists decide that air, earth and fire were not really elements at all.
5. The Earth pulls on all objects with a force of gravity (   ).
6. My adviser will have been teaching for forty years (   ).
7. Most of the undergraduate students in the Faculty of Global Studies study abroad (   ).
8. All the classes during the first period are required to start (   ).
9. (   ) were wriggling angleworms.
10. Lithium batteries are prohibited to be sent (   ).

a. by air in many countries
b. by the end of the school year
c. at the beginning of the year
d. until the end of October
e. not until the eighteenth century
f. since April 5, 2009, on the QBS Television Network
g. during their second year
h. under piles of leaves
i. downward, that is, toward the center of the Earth
j. on time, at 9:00 in the morning

Writing Assignments

Writing a Spatial Order Paragraph

A Ask your partner questions about his or her room to learn where things are located, and draw a picture of it.

B Write a short paragraph about your partner's room based on the picture you drew in **A** above.

C Examine the campus map of a university below and write a paragraph describing the layout of the campus.

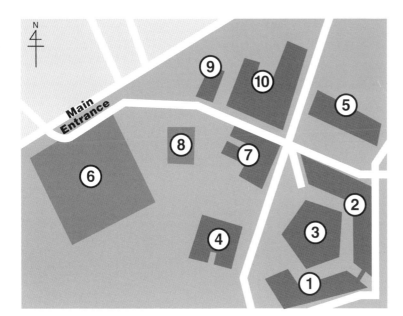

① Engineering Lecture Hall
② Sciences Lab Building
③ Library
④ Physical Activities Complex
⑤ Administrative Building
⑥ Playing Field
⑦ Student Life Center
⑧ Parking Facility
⑨ Health Services Building
⑩ Research Center

Unit 4

Amazing Inventions

Quick Survey Ask the following five questions to your partner. Then, write your answers, your partner's answers, and the most popular answers in your group or class.

Question	Your answer	Your partner's answer	Most popular answer
1. Is state-of-the-art technology essential to you?			
2. What kind of technology do you depend on?			
3. How much do you depend on technology?			
4. Do you use the internet every day?			
5. Why do you use the internet?			

Dialog 11

Victor is listening to music with his smartphone when he suddenly takes off his earphones.

Victor: It's funny…

Kimi: What's up?

Victor: You know, we use MP3 players like the iPod, and we don't really even think about it. This kind of technology just seems ordinary and normal to us.

5 **Kimi:** That's true. We have the internet, many different kinds of electronic devices, etc., and we never really stop to consider how amazing these inventions are.

Victor: Yeah, I never think about it. Just imagine how surprised people probably were when they heard recorded sound for the first time! I guess people must have been really shocked.

10 **Kimi:** Are you talking about Edison's greatest invention, the phonograph?

Victor: I am. I think Edison is the greatest inventor of all time.

Kimi:	Yeah, quite possibly. It is amazing that he was able to think of a way to put sound onto a thing, and then play it back. He had an idea that sound could be recorded, and then invented a device which could actually do it. Incredible!
15 **Victor:**	That is unbelievable.
Kimi:	I believe that he realized how important his invention was.
Victor:	Edison developed many important technologies, such as the first high quality electric light bulb, electric power generation and distribution, and of course, the phonograph.
Kimi:	That's impressive. However, I'm most impressed by the fact that he made thousands of models and failed many times before he finally succeeded in creating finished products.
Victor:	Persistence pays off. I feel that this is the most important lesson we can gain from his work.
Kimi:	Yeah, I agree. His work is very inspiring. Edison also introduced the kinetoscope, didn't he? I know it was one of the first machines developed which could record motion pictures.
Victor:	If you're interested, you can see the earliest recorded movies on the website of the Library of Congress. Here, I'll show you. *(He shows her his phone.)*
Kimi:	Wow. This movie seems really old.
Victor:	It was recorded using Edison's amazing invention in 1894.
30 **Kimi:**	More than 100 years ago! He is the father of modern entertainment. What an extraordinary man.

Exercises   Dialog Summary

Part 1 Dictation 🎧 12

Listen and fill in the blanks.

Victor (　　　　) his thoughts with Kimi. They talk about how amazing inventions are all around them. For example, Thomas Edison developed a lot of incredible devices. Victor (　　　　) (　　　　) (　　　　) must have been shocked when they heard (　　　　) (　　　　) for the first time. Next, they talk about Edison's inventions, (　　　　) the first high quality electric light bulb, electric power (　　　　) and (　　　　), and the (　　　　).

Part 2 Dictation 🎧 13

Listen and fill in the blanks.

Victor and Kimi agree that there are truly amazing inventions all around them, although they have never thought about it before. In particular, they are focusing on Thomas Edison. Victor feels that people must have been really shocked when they first heard recorded sound. Next, they talk about the fact that Edison was involved in many inventions, including the first high quality electric light bulb, electric power generation and distribution, and the phonograph. In addition, they are impressed by the fact that Edison failed many times before his eventual success. Finally, they discuss the (　　　　), which was also (　　　　) (　　　　) Edison. It was one of the first machines which could record (　　　　) (　　　　). Kimi shares her opinion that Edison is the father of (　　　　) (　　　　).

Part 3 Writing a summary

Answer the following questions and then write a summary of the dialog.

1. What comes to Victor's mind when he's using his smartphone?

   _____

2. According to the dialog, what is the most important lesson one can gain from Edison's work?

   _____

3. Which inventions do they discuss?

   _____

28

Amazing Inventions

Grammar Focus — Verbs Related to Perception

Synonyms for "think" are used in different situations. The verbs related to perception conveying thought, emotion, and sense are not usually used in progressive forms. Verbs such as appear, look, hear, feel, smell, sound, and taste can be used as linking verbs and are often followed by an adjective or noun.

Choose a verb from the box below to complete each of the following sentences. Change its form and tense if necessary. Use a capital letter to begin the first word of each sentence.

1. Some people (   ) in God, a notion that can be controversial in science.

2. There are many ways to choose a computer password that is hard for hackers to (   ).

3. We (   ) to cultivate professionals with a broad perspective to help solve environmental problems.

4. I can't (   ) a world without refrigerators in summer. This technology is necessary in modern society.

5. He was able to (   ) the topic of the book by looking at its cover. It's about a particle accelerator.

6. When Isaac Newton discovered the law of gravity, he (   ) its monumental importance.

7. (   ) we plan to roll two dice and we're interested in the sum of the two numbers appearing on the top faces.

8. Sulfur (   ) bad. It's like rotten eggs.

9. Humpback whale song (   ) familiar to me. I think I've heard it before, but I'm not sure.

10. Dinosaurs became extinct. However, most of the large members of the cat family, which (   ) endangered, can be saved if we take action.

| appear | believe | guess | hope | imagine |
| infer | realize | smell | sound | suppose |

Unit 4

Writing Assignments — Writing a Descriptive Paragraph (1)

A Ask your partner about a famous person he or she admires, and why.

B Write a short paragraph about a person your partner respects, based on your partner's response in **A** above.

C Write a paragraph about a famous figure you greatly admire, and explain what he or she is like using as many adjectives and adjective phrases as possible.

Adjectives of positive factors to describe people who you like or admire:

appealing	charismatic	magnetic	
artistic	creative		
handsome	pretty	attractive	good-looking
elegant	sophisticated		
gifted	talented	skilled	
nice	sweet	pleasant	
empathetic	considerate		
successful	prosperous		
brave	courageous		
affectionate	loving	caring	compassionate
hardworking	industrious		
intelligent	smart	brilliant	
honorable	respectable	admirable	
mysterious	enchanting		
reliable	dependable	responsible	
funny	witty	hilarious	
fit	in good shape		
warm	friendly	genial	

*Words in horizontal rows have a similar meaning.

Unit 5 The Sun Is White

Quick Survey

Ask the following five questions to your partner. Then, write your answers, your partner's answers, and the most popular answers in your group or class.

Question	Your answer	Your partner's answer	Most popular answer
1. Are you interested in astronomy?			
2. Are you interested in photography?			
3. What kind of device do you usually use when you take a photograph?			
4. Do you like to have your picture taken?			
5. What is the best photo you have ever taken? When did you take it?			

Dialog 14

Shun sees Serena watching the sunset alone. He thinks that it is a good opportunity to have a conversation, so he approaches her.

Shun: Hey, what's up?

Serena: Not too much. I was just checking out the sunset. It sure is gorgeous.

Shun: You know, I have a telescope at home. I really enjoy astrophotography. Sometimes, I use my scope to take pictures of the sun.

5 **Serena:** Can you show me one of your photos?

Shun: Sure, I'd be happy to. Here's a photo of the sun. I took it last weekend at around 10:00 a.m.

Serena: That's pretty cool, but the sun looks white. It's a black and white photo, right? Can I see the color version?

10 **Shun:** This is a color photo. In fact, the sun is white. It's not yellow, orange, or red. It's white.

Serena: No way! I don't believe you.

Shun: Actually, when the sun is overhead, it appears white, but we can't look at it directly because it's too dangerous and it hurts our eyes.

Serena: OK, maybe that's true when the sun is directly overhead. But sunsets and sunrises are always so colorful.

Shun: When the sun is on the horizon, it appears orange, red or yellow because of dust and other materials in our atmosphere.

Serena: Isn't it dangerous to take a picture of the sun?

Shun: No, it isn't, if you take the proper precautions. I can attach a device to my telescope called a Herschel wedge to make it safer. Then, I put a special filter into the Herschel wedge to cut most of the light, so the sun is easier to view.

Serena: That's why the background is so dark in your photo.

Shun: That's exactly right. The filter is dark, so the sky background looks dark. However, the sun is so bright that you can see it through the filter, at a comfortable level of brightness.

Serena: Near the bottom of the sun in your photo, I see some dark spots. Are they sunspots?

Shun: Yeah, they are. They are caused by magnetic activity on the sun.

Serena: Why do they look black?

Shun: In fact, they aren't black. They are much brighter than the full moon! However, they are cooler in temperature than the areas around them, so they appear dark.

Serena: That makes sense.

Exercises Dialog Summary

Part 1 Dictation 🎧 15

Listen and fill in the blanks.

   Shun shows Serena a photograph. Serena (   ) (   ) because she thinks it's a black and white picture, but actually it's a color photo of the sun. The photo (   ) that the sun is white. In fact, when it's overhead, it appears white, but we can't look at it directly because it's dangerous and (   ) our eyes. Shun takes the photo using a Herschel wedge with an installed filter, so the sun is easier and safer (   ) (   ).

Part 2 Dictation 🎧 16

Listen and fill in the blanks.

   Serena is shown a picture. It's a color photo of the sun. The sun is white, which (   ) Serena. It (   ) white when it's overhead, but it's too dangerous for our eyes to look at it directly. When on the horizon, the sun appears orange, red or yellow because of dust and other materials in our atmosphere. Shun takes the photo (   ) (   ) (   ) a Herschel wedge and a filter. A few sunspots (   ) by magnetic activity on the sun can be (   ) in the photo. In fact, those sunspots are (   ) brighter than the full moon, but they look dark (   ) (   ) (   ) (   ) in temperature (   ) (   ) (   ) the areas around them.

Part 3 Writing a summary

Answer the following questions and then write a summary of the dialog.

1. Can you describe the photo that Shun shows Serena?

   _____

2. What precautions does Shun need to take in order to take a picture of the sun?

   _____

3. Why do sunspots look black?

   _____

Grammar Focus: Adjectives and Adjective Clauses

Adjectives describe a noun or pronoun. An adjective clause contains a subject and verb, and begins with a relative pronoun: who, whom, whose, that, or which, or a relative adverb: when, where, or why. These clauses modify nouns.

A Choose a word from the box below to complete each of the following sentences.

1. A laser is a(n) (   ) device that produces a narrow, intense (   ) light.

2. Scientists perform research toward a more (   ) understanding of nature, including (   ), mathematical and social realms.

3. Most airplanes are flown by a pilot on board the aircraft, but some are designed to be (   ) or computer-controlled.

4. Algebra is the study of operations and their application to (   ) equations.

5. The Tiger Swallowtail butterfly is a strong flier with (   ) yellow and black (   ) markings on its wings and body.

advanced	coherent	comprehensive	distinctive
physical	remotely	solving	striped

B Choose a phrase from the box below to complete each adjective clause in the following sentences.

1. The students will participate in a scientific experiment (   ) retain water in order for them to survive in hot, dry parts of the world.

2. A scientist is a person (   ) of the natural sciences.

3. Stability and control are much more complex for an airplane (   ) in three dimensions, than for cars or boats which only move in two.

4. International mathematics courses contain a body of knowledge (   ) and apply, ranging from algebra concepts, statistics, and geometry, to trigonometry and differential calculus.

5. The biggest living creature (   ) right now may be the blue whale.

a. that scientists know of	d. who studies one or more
b. that shows how cacti	e. which can move freely
c. which students are required to learn	

Writing Assignments — Writing a Descriptive Paragraph (2)

A Ask your partner to describe his or her favorite possession, and draw a picture of it.

B Write a short paragraph about your partner's favorite possession.

C Look at the picture and description of the smartphone below. Then, write a paragraph describing your phone, using as many adjectives as possible.

Design:
  eye-catching

Body:
  lightweight aluminum

Camera and video:
  low-light, exclusive digital lenses, high resolution, wide viewing angle

Screen:
  glass, easy to clean, super-sensitive touch screen technology

E-mail and messaging:
  viewing and editing of e-mail attachments

Call management:
  incredible noise cancellation

Music and audio:
  great sound quality, almost unlimited number of songs

Battery life:
  long lasting, outstanding

The order of adjectives for describing high-tech gadgets:

size	shape	color	origin	material	characteristics	function
small	cubic	black	Korean	aluminum	advanced	artificial
medium	square	white	Chinese	carbon fiber	innovative	cybernetic
large	circular	pink	Japanese	glass	modern	hypertext-based
long	triangular	red	American	plastic	state-of-the-art	interactive
short	elliptical	blue	Swiss	steel	conductive	multipurpose
big	oval	transparent	Taiwanese	titanium	insulative	multifunctional
compact	boxy	translucent			analog	voice-activated
tiny		opaque			digital	memory-expandable
					solar-powered	broadband
					wireless	dial-up
					rechargeable	video chat
					user-friendly	high-definition
					powerful	cloud
					versatile	backup

Unit 6 Online Social Networking

Quick Survey Ask the following five questions to your partner. Then, write your answers, your partner's answers, and the most popular answers in your group or class.

Question	Your answer	Your partner's answer	Most popular answer
1. Do you use an online social networking service?			
2. How often do you use one?			
3. Why do you think people use online social networking services?			
4. Do you feel that it's necessary to join one?			
5. Would you like to use the internet less often?			

Dialog 17

Taro and Serena are in a school cafeteria. All of the people around them are staring at their phones, sending and receiving text messages.

Taro: No one is talking! Everyone's just staring at their phones. Is it the same way in your country?

Serena: Yeah, in libraries, restaurants, on trains, everywhere, people are text messaging. It seems that they are always using the internet or an online social networking service.

5 **Taro:** Well, me too, but I do try to avoid using it at home. This kind of technology is making people into internet addicts. I don't want to be addicted.

Serena: Although it's addictive, I have to admit, it really is amazing. Even though I'm here in Japan, I can communicate with my friends and family in the United States so easily with e-mail and instant messaging.

10 **Taro:** I get to see my friends and family almost every day, so I guess I don't need to

	communicate with them online quite as often.
Serena:	Well, because I'm so far away from home, this kind of technology really helps me a lot. I imagine that it would be very difficult to live abroad without it.
Taro:	I see. It sounds like it's changed your life for the better.
15 Serena:	It has. However, of course, I don't think it's healthy for people to actually stop talking to other people.
Taro:	That's true. Face-to-face communication, and time spent away from the internet, are both also important!
Serena:	I agree. You know, online communication has become so prevalent that it's almost impossible to imagine the world without it. Do you know when people started to use the internet?
Taro:	Well, I don't major in computer science, so I'm not an expert… but I do know that computers were developed in the 1950s, the first operational packet-switching network was developed in the 1960s and 1970s, and the World Wide Web was created in the early 1990s.
Serena:	My father has always loved new technology. He told me that he started to use online social networking services in the mid-1990s.
Taro:	That makes sense.
Serena:	Why?
30 Taro:	Although the internet advanced during the 1980s, it wasn't until the advent of the World Wide Web that it really found widespread use in the general population.

Exercises Dialog Summary

Part 1 Dictation 🎧 18

Listen and fill in the blanks.

   Students in a school cafeteria are staring at their phones. It seems that they are using the internet. Perhaps they are using a (   ) (   ) (   ). Taro and Serena say that this kind of technology is (   ) people into (   ) (   ). Serena thinks it's amazing that she can communicate with her friends and family in the United States so easily with e-mail and (   ) (   ). She also thinks that this technology really helps her a lot because she's so (   ) (   ) from home. Serena asks Taro about the time when people started to use the internet. He explains that computers were developed in the 1950s, the first operational packet-switching network was developed in the 1960s and 1970s, and the (   ) (   ) (   ) was created in the early 1990s.

Part 2 Dictation 🎧 19

Listen and fill in the blanks.

   Students in a school cafeteria appear to be using the internet. Perhaps they are checking an online social networking service. Taro and Serena discuss the idea that this kind of technology is making people into internet addicts. Serena is happy that she can communicate with her friends and family in the United States so easily with e-mail and instant messaging, even though it's addictive. (   ) Taro doesn't need to communicate with (   ) friends and family (   ) (   ) (   ) because he sees them almost every day, Serena thinks that the technology is very helpful to her because she's (   ) (   ) (   ) (   ) (   ) (   ). However, Serena thinks it's (   ) for people to stop talking to other people and Taro thinks face-to-face communication and time away from the internet are also important. Finally, in reply to Serena's question, Taro talks about the history of the internet. He discusses the (   ) (   ) (   ) in the 1950s, the first operational packet-switching network in the 1960s and 1970s, and the creation of the World Wide Web in the early 1990s. Serena's father started to use online social networking services in the mid-1990s. Taro isn't surprised by this because the advent of the World Wide Web played an important role in making internet use more widespread in the (   ) (   ).

Part 3 Writing a summary

Answer the following questions and then write a summary of the dialog.

1. What type of addiction do they discuss?
   _____

2. What do Serena and Taro think about the power of the internet?
   _____

3. How does Taro reply to Serena's question regarding the time when people began to use the internet?
   _____

Grammar Focus Nouns and Noun Clauses

> A noun is a word or phrase that represents a person, animal, place, thing, or idea. It can be used as an object of a verb or preposition, and can be the subject of a sentence. Because a noun clause functions as a noun, it can also be used as an object or the subject in a sentence.

Complete each of the following sentences with an appropriate word.

1. The group members discussed (   ) or not they should focus on biological research.
   a. what   **b.** it   **c.** either   **d.** whether

2. Your report is a useful record of (   ) you observed in the laboratory.
   a. what   **b.** it   **c.** that   **d.** whether

3. This document describes (   ) the plans meet the needs of the community.
   a. it   **b.** how   **c.** when   **d.** what

4. (   ) happened in the spacecraft was a tragedy.
   a. What   **b.** How   **c.** When   **d.** Whether

5. My father remembers (   ) his first computer was brought home.
   a. what   **b.** where   **c.** when   **d.** whether

6. (   ) works the hardest has the best chance to succeed.
   a. Whatever   **b.** Whoever   **c.** Whenever   **d.** Whichever

7. Some scientific evidence proves (   ) the planet is getting warmer.
   a. what   b. which   c. when   d. that

8. (   ) moon rotates on its axis in approximately the same amount of time it takes to orbit the Earth.
   a. A   b. One   c. Each   d. The

9. Nobody passed the physics exam, did (   )?
   a. it   b. that   c. he   d. they

10. I saw my math professor near the station yesterday. Today, I saw (   ) same professor near the station again.
    a. a   b. one   c. each   d. the

Writing Assignments — Writing a Sequential Order Paragraph

A Ask your partner about his or her first experience using a computer, including feelings about the experience, the approximate date when it happened, etc.

B Write a short paragraph about your partner's first experience using a computer, based on the response in **A** above. Events should be discussed in sequential order.

C Write a paragraph about your first experience using a computer. Events should be discussed in sequential order.

Unit 7: Robotic Cleaner

Quick Survey — Ask the following five questions to your partner. Then, write your answers, your partner's answers, and the most popular answers in your group or class.

Question	Your answer	Your partner's answer	Most popular answer
1. Would you like to have a robot at home?			
2. Are you interested in studying robotics?			
3. What type of robots would you like to create?			
4. What kinds of jobs would you like them to do?			
5. Would you like to run a company?			

Dialog 20

> Victor and his friends are working on a project in his apartment. An automated robotic vacuum cleaner is moving around the floor. Serena is staring at it.

Serena: Is it any good? I wonder if it can really replace the traditional vacuum cleaner.

Victor: Yeah, it really is good. It cleans the room perfectly. It covers the whole floor, and it can go everywhere. It can detect and vacuum dirt even when it's under the furniture.

Serena: What does it do when something is blocking it?

5 **Victor:** When it comes to an obstacle, it changes direction. I didn't believe it at first, but when I learned that it was created by an advanced technology company, rather than a typical consumer electronics maker, I got interested. I bought it in America.

Taro: Oh, it's the same company that creates the robots which are used to gather data at a nuclear disaster site, right?

10 **Victor:** Yeah, and another one of their robots also took an active role after a particularly large

	and damaging oil spill.
Ari:	That's cool. Wow, now it's returning to its docking station.
Victor:	It returns to recharge after finishing its cleaning cycle. It's powered by a rechargeable battery.
15 Taro:	It seems to have similar sensors to a robotic dog. Do you know about robotic dogs?
Victor:	Yeah, I do! In fact, this kind of technology can be adapted to perform various tasks.
Serena:	I imagine that it would be very useful for people with disabilities.
Ari:	It is. Cleaning is a really difficult task for the elderly and people who are sick.
Taro:	They're still expensive, though. That's the problem.
20 Victor:	Actually, it does sell pretty well. As more companies enter the marketplace with similar robots, they'll become cheaper.
Taro:	Hey, I have an idea. Let's get together and create a new type of robot someday.
Victor:	Fantastic!
Ari:	That sounds exciting! Let's work it out.
25 Serena:	Before doing that, don't you think it would be a good idea for us to finish our homework first?
Victor:	No question.

Exercises Dialog Summary

Part 1 Dictation 🎧 21

Listen and fill in the blanks.

Serena asks Victor if the (   ) robotic vacuum cleaner can really (   ) a traditional (   ). Victor says that it cleans the room (   ). He says that when it (   ) to an obstacle, it changes direction. When he learned that the robot was created by an (   ) technology company, he (   ) interested, and then he bought it in America. Taro says that the company also creates robots which are used to gather data at a (   ) (   ) (   ).

Part 2 Dictation 🎧 22

Listen and fill in the blanks.

Serena asks Victor if the automated robotic vacuum cleaner can actually replace a traditional one. Victor says that it cleans the room very well, and it changes direction when it approaches an obstacle. When he found out that the robot was developed by an advanced technology company, he bought one. Taro shares that the company also makes robots which gather data at a nuclear disaster site. Victor adds that their other robots took an active role after a particularly large and damaging (   ) (   ). He says that the robotic cleaner is powered by a (   ) (   ) and thus returns to its docking station after finishing the cleaning cycle. This kind of robot can be useful for people for whom cleaning is a difficult task, such as (   ) (   ) (   ) (   ) (   ). However, they are expensive and thus some people (   ) (   ) them.

Part 3 Writing a summary

Answer the following questions and then write a summary of the dialog.

1. Why does Victor buy a robotic vacuum cleaner?

   _____

2. What information do Taro and Victor discuss regarding the company that produces the robot?

   _____

3. Who benefits from this type of technology?

   _____

Grammar Focus — Nouns—Countable / Uncountable

When a noun is used, it is important to determine if it is countable or uncountable. If uncountable, the noun refers to something that cannot be counted (a mass), and so it does not use a plural form. When a noun is countable and it refers to only one person, place or thing, the singular form is used. If the noun refers to more than one, we use the plural form. Plurals are usually created by adding -s to a noun's singular form, but the spelling of plurals varies and can be irregular.

Complete each of the following sentences with an appropriate word or phrase.

1. Donating blood is a good way to save a life because patients often require (   ) or platelets to help treat a fatal disease.
   a. a blood   b. was blood   c. blood   d. its

2. Radiation, matter, gravitation, electric charge, and magnetism are all invisible physical (   ).
   a. a phenomenon   b. phenomenon   c. the phenomenons   d. phenomena

3. If people have (   ) lasting a week or longer, it may be caused by the flu.
   a. fever   b. a fever   c. fevers   d. the fevers

4. The (   ) are using the forensic science lab report to help them in the investigation.
   a. detective   b. police officer   c. polices   d. police

5. (   ) travels in straight lines, and transmits energy from one place to another.
   a. Light   b. The lights   c. A light   d. Lights

6. Although (   ) people think that smoking is healthy, some people do think that smoking is a relaxing tool. Surprisingly, (   ) people never try to quit smoking.
   a. quite a little, little   b. little, quite a few   c. few, quite a few   d. quite a few, little

7. (   ) in the summer camp are interested in nature.
   a. Most of childs   b. The most child   c. Most of children   d. Most of the children

8. Taking (   ) can be dangerous if you don't recognize an adverse reaction.
   a. medicine   b. a medicine   c. medicines   d. one medicine

9. Electronic data exchange via e-mail or the Web is more eco-friendly than using millions of (   ).
   a. a sheet of paper   b. a sheet of papers   c. sheets of paper   d. sheets of papers

10. (   ) of the employees in the company are contract workers.
    a. Lot   b. Half   c. Number   d. Majority

Writing Assignments — Writing a Definitive Paragraph

A Ask your partner about what kind of robot he or she might like to build, and why.

B Write a short paragraph about the robot your partner described in **A** above.

C Write a paragraph about your ideal robot. Include reasons and details in your answer.

Unit 8: Water Survey

Quick Survey

Ask the following five questions to your partner. Then, write your answers, your partner's answers, and the most popular answers in your group or class.

Question	Your answer	Your partner's answer	Most popular answer
1. What kinds of experiments do you enjoy doing?			
2. Can you name different types of pollution?			
3. Are you interested in helping to keep the environment clean?			
4. Do you try to do something environmentally friendly every day?			
5. Do you do anything that hurts the environment?			

Dialog 23

Students are conducting an experiment to analyze water pollution for an independent project. They are using a water monitoring kit in a laboratory. First, they collected samples in five different locations from the river near their university. The cups of water have been sorted into five test tubes. They finish plotting, and start analyzing.

Water Temperature	25 °C	Nitrate	3.6 mg/L
Coliform Bacteria	13,000 MPN/100 mL	Phosphate	0.12 mg/L
Dissolved Oxygen	8.3 mg/L	pH	7.6
Biochemical Oxygen Demand	2.9 mg/L	Suspended Solids	12 mg/L

Ari: Let's start with the water temperature.

Victor: It's slightly above average for this time of year.

Kimi:	How about the coliform bacteria?
Ryoma:	Positive. The rate is rather high, which is disturbing. There's no indication of the cause.
Ari:	How's the dissolved oxygen?
Ryoma:	Moderate.
Victor:	What can you tell me about the biochemical dissolved oxygen?
Ari:	The level is a little high, which indicates that it's polluted. And how about the nitrate and phosphate?
Victor:	Fair. It's probably nothing to be overly concerned about, but I'd like to continue collecting data on this.
Kimi:	OK. The pH level is a bit higher than the level we tested it at last month, but still well within the normal range. And what's the last one?
Victor:	Turbidity. Lower turbidity means higher water clarity, so there's nothing to be concerned about regarding this test.
Ryoma:	And that's it, we're done.
Ari:	Have you ever tried a similar experiment in your country?
Victor:	I have. I took part in a water quality study of the Hudson River.
Ryoma:	Is the Hudson River in New York?
Victor:	Yeah, it's in New York State. It starts at a point way north, past Albany, and then flows south all the way to New Jersey.
Kimi:	I see. Does the Hudson have any major problems?
Victor:	Well, there is some PCB contamination. In 1977, PCBs were banned in the US, but before that time they were used and caused some damage.
Ari:	I've read that Japan had a similar situation, and also banned their use in the 1970s. We are fortunate, at least, that now we understand the mistakes of the past and can work to correct them.
Victor:	Indeed. The government, researchers, advocates, and even students have been working together on a cleanup campaign for the river. It's really been effective so far. However, it seems that the results vary depending on the location, season, and other factors.
Ari:	So, it's important to continue monitoring. What we're doing is essential.
Victor:	That's true! Let's proceed with our work.

Exercises Dialog Summary

Part 1 [Dictation] 🎧 24

Listen and fill in the blanks.

    Students (   ) (   ) an experiment to analyze water pollution. They plot a diagram, and start by analyzing the water temperature. They proceed to analyze the coliform bacteria, dissolved oxygen, biochemical oxygen demand, nitrate, phosphate, pH, and suspended solids. Victor says that he helped to (   ) a (   ) experiment in (   ) country, a (   ) (   ) study of New York's Hudson River. There is some (   ) (   ) in the river, which is a major problem. In 1977, PCBs were banned in the US. Japan had a similar situation and also banned their use in the 1970s.

Part 2 [Dictation] 🎧 25

Listen and fill in the blanks.

    Students (   ) an experiment to analyze water pollution. They plot and analyze each of the following items, in order: water temperature, coliform bacteria, dissolved oxygen, biochemical oxygen demand, nitrate, phosphate, pH, and suspended solids. It is disturbing that the rate of (   ) (   ) (   ) (   ) and rather high even though there's no (   ) of the (   ). After finishing the analysis, they discuss Victor's (   ) in a similar water quality study of the Hudson River in New York. The river was contaminated by PCBs. This was (   ) to be a major problem, and PCBs were banned in the US in 1977. Japan banned their use in the 1970s due to a similar situation. (   ) (   ) Victor, a number of people including politicians, researchers, advocates, and students have been joining a cleanup campaign for the river, which has been effective (   ) (   ). However, it seems that the results are (   ), depending on (   ) (   ) location and season.

Part 3 [Writing a summary]

Answer the following questions and then write a summary of the dialog.

1. What do the students do in the lab? In what order do they analyze the items?

　_____

2. What do they discuss after their analysis is finished?

　_____

3. What is a major problem of the Hudson River?

_____

Grammar Focus — Verb Forms (2)

> As we have seen in Unit 2, some verbs may be followed by gerunds, but others can be followed by infinitives. In addition to this, different verbs can take different definite structures. Some verbs can be used in a passive structure of a sentence.

Complete each of the following sentences with an appropriate word or phrase.

1. There are various things you can do to (   ) protect the environment.
   a. have   b. make   c. help   d. do

2. The software corporation (   ) users to take advantage of the latest software updates until the next version is released.
   a. allows   b. has   c. lets   d. tends

3. In Australia, you may (   ) to see a large herd of kangaroos.
   a. allow   b. happen   c. cause   d. let

4. To keep the computer network in good working order, professionals recommend that we (   ) having regular server updates.
   a. attempt   b. decide   c. consider   d. ask

5. Because of their nature, water molecules at the surface (   ) separating.
   a. drive   b. cause   c. resist   d. refuse

6. A strong wind blew in, and even the heavy metallic door of the lab (   ) behind me.
   a. closed   b. to be closing c. have closed   d. will be closed

7. Sagrada Família is a large, famous Roman Catholic church in Barcelona, and (   ) by architect Antoni Gaudí.
   a. designed   b. is designed   c. was designed d. to design

8. We (   ) someone next door in the dormitory crying through the night.
   a. heard   b. thought   c. considered   d. admitted

9. I'm always hesitant about having my photo (   ) or asking someone to take a picture of me while taking part in a poster session at an academic conference.
   a. take   b. to take   c. taking   d. taken

10. There (　　　　) to be light snow and fog at the time when the plane accident happened.
 a. report **b.** reported **c.** was reported **d.** has reported

Writing Assignments   Writing a Process Analysis Paragraph

A Ask your partner about the most interesting experiment that he or she has ever done, and why.

B Write a short paragraph about an interesting experiment, based on your partner's response in **A** above.

C Write a paragraph about the most interesting experiment that you've ever done, and explain why.

Unit 9 Optical Illusions

Quick Survey Ask the following five questions to your partner. Then, write your answers, your partner's answers, and the most popular answers in your group or class.

Question	Your answer	Your partner's answer	Most popular answer
1. Have you ever seen the optical illusions depicted in this unit?			
2. Have you ever seen any other optical illusions?			
3. Do you have good eyesight?			
4. Do you easily notice imperfections in things?			
5. Have you ever been fooled by an illusion?			

Dialog 26

Victor hasn't decided what topic he'll use for a presentation next week. Victor sees Ari working on something, and it seems that it's related to the presentation.

Victor: Have you decided on a topic for the presentation next Friday?

Ari: I was searching the internet for some good ideas, and I've finally figured it out. I'll talk about optical illusions.

Victor: What's an optical illusion?

5 Ari: Optical illusions occur when the information gathered by our eyes is perceived by the brain in a way which is different from reality. Here's an example. *(She shows him her smartphone.)*

Victor: Hmm, I think I've seen this before... is it a famous example?

10 Ari: Yes, it is probably the most famous example. The lines

	appear to bend and move, but in fact they are straight and of course they are perfectly still.
Victor:	This reminds me of another picture I've seen. In that picture, it's unclear if you are looking at a vase, or two people staring at each other.
15 **Ari:**	*(She shows another picture on her smartphone to him.)* You mean this one?
Victor:	Yeah, that one, exactly. Both pictures create an illusion, but the effect in this one is somehow different from the first one you showed me. I also think it's a much better, more interesting 20 illusion.
Ari:	There are thought to be three categories of illusions, but it seems there's no widely accepted notion. There could be even more categories. Anyway, of these two, some say the former is a physiological illusion, while the latter is a cognitive illusion. However, others say both are examples of a cognitive 25 illusion.
Victor:	The fields of research needed to create and study these illusions must be different, and pretty complicated.
Ari:	You can say that again. It's even more complicated than most people think.
Victor:	It sounds to me that physiological illusions must be dependent on the brain's past 30 experience of interacting with the world. On the other hand, cognitive illusions must be more dependent on unconscious inferences.
Ari:	You're probably right. There is also another type of optical illusion. This type of illusion is usually created by an artist, and the images often 35 combine different types of common objects to produce something entirely different. *(She shows the third picture to him.)* Look at this picture.
Victor:	Wow! What is this? That's the best one I've seen so far!
40 **Ari:**	An artist created a picture of a woman looking at a mirror, but her head and its reflection can also be perceived as the eyes of a skull.
Victor:	I see. I saw a similar picture, in which different types of fruits are combined to form a man's face and torso.
45 **Ari:**	That's fascinating. These images truly help us to perceive the world in a new way. Looking at them is certainly more fun than simply reading about them!

Exercises Dialog Summary

Part 1 Dictation 🎧 27

Listen and fill in the blanks.

Ari tells Victor that she (   ) optical illusions as the (   ) for her presentation next Friday. When our eyes perceive something in a way which (   ) from reality, it's an optical illusion. She shows Victor a picture in which the lines appear to bend and move. Victor is (   ) of another picture he has seen, in which both a vase and two people staring at each other can be seen. Victor (   ) that the two illusions are somehow different.

Part 2 Dictation 🎧 28

Listen and fill in the blanks.

Ari tells Victor about some of the optical illusions she will discuss during her presentation next Friday. She talks about the (   ) of an optical illusion, and then shows Victor a picture as an example. In her example, the lines (   ) (   ) (   ) they bend and move. Victor then remembers another picture he has seen which includes both a vase and two people staring at each other. There are even more types of illusions. Victor tries to explain the (   ) between two types of illusions: a physiological illusion and a cognitive illusion. Ari proceeds to show Victor a third type of optical illusion, created by an artist. She says that optical illusions are (   ) for us to perceive the world in a new way, and looking at them is more fun than reading about them.

Part 3 Writing a summary

Answer the following questions and then write a summary of the dialog.

1. How does Ari describe the first optical illusion that she shows Victor?

2. What does Victor say about the illusion?

3. What does Ari think that optical illusions help us to do?

Optical Illusions

Grammar Focus — Comparative and Superlative Adjectives

> There are various ways to compare two or more things, but the most common is to use comparative and superlative adjectives and adverbs. There are both regular forms and irregular forms. Comparative and superlative adjectives are modified with adverbs such as much, far, and even, rather than the adverb, "very."

Choose a word or phrase from the box below to complete each of the following sentences. Change its form if necessary.

1. Warm water holds (   ) oxygen than cold water.
2. The more you learn, the (   ) you realize how little you know.
3. Fraternal twins are (   ) than identical twins.
4. Students are required to do as (   ) math exercises as possible and upload them to the website before the due date of the assignment.
5. Some economists estimate that the demand for electricity grows almost (   ) as fast as the total amount of energy consumption.
6. The more energy an object has, the (   ) it will be.
7. Human brains are (   ) more complex than people previously thought.
8. Sundials were (   ) the most well-known timekeeping devices in earlier times.
9. The tallest building in the world is only about (   ) taller than a certain type of tree.
10. Neil Armstrong was the (   ) man to walk on the moon.

a lot	by far	common	first	four times
heavy	little	many	much	twice

Writing Assignments
Writing a Comparison or Contrast Paragraph

A Compare your phone to your partner's phone. Discuss how they compare or contrast in their appearance and function.

B Write a short paragraph about the similarity between your phone and your partner's phone, based on your discussion in **A** above. You may use these words: like, similar to, alike, the same as.

C Write a paragraph which compares an old version and the latest version of your favorite electronic device. Explain which one is recommended, and how they differ from each other. Use as many comparative and superlative expressions as possible. You may also use these words: unlike, different from, differ.

Unit 10 School Planning and Design

Quick Survey — Ask the following five questions to your partner. Then, write your answers, your partner's answers, and the most popular answers in your group or class.

Question	Your answer	Your partner's answer	Most popular answer
1. What are two of your strongest memories from elementary school?			
2. In your opinion, what are the characteristics of a great building?			
3. Please name a famous building, and describe how it looks.			
4. Would you rather live in the city, or the suburbs?			
5. Do you feel that including "green spaces" in urban areas is important?			

Dialog 29

> Architecture is related to many different fields. Therefore, this class is open to students from all departments.

Prof. Terada: What should we consider when we undertake elementary school planning and design?

Students: *(murmuring excitedly amongst themselves)*

Prof. Terada: Let's start with the school's location. Elementary school students in Japan usually go to school on foot. How might that influence our decision about where to build it?

Kimi: I think school buildings should not be built near main traffic arteries, so we can reduce the possibility of dangerous accidents. Being sufficiently apart from roads and streets is also an effective strategy to minimize traffic noise, which can be a nuisance to classes.

Victor: In my opinion, it's better for schools to be built in suburban areas. Elementary

	schools should have a lot of playground space. Perhaps they should also be built near forests and parks, so the students have the opportunity to interact with nature.
Serena:	On the other hand, if undeveloped areas are used, trees need to be cleared. That would be destructive to the environment.
Prof. Terada:	Those are all worthwhile observations. We do have to be careful not to damage the environment, even if the cleared space would result in a larger play area for children. Let's move on to the next step. Imagine that we have to build a school building in a city, very close to busy roads. We don't have much space to work with. What should our biggest concerns be?
Kimi:	We must find a way to block most of the noise. We should also consider the structure's compatibility with the local environment, including the ability to withstand strong storms. We need really solid walls.
Victor:	Criminals may hide in dark areas. Both the school's interior and grounds should be kept well lit at all times.
Serena:	We have to protect children from airborne pollutants. Plants would help to screen them out.
Victor:	I agree, that's a good idea, and I think we should include flowers. They are beautiful, and taking care of them could be a fun project for the students. Flowers would really help to create a comfortable atmosphere for adults and children alike.
Kimi:	And if we put some flowers near the entrance of the school, it would really help to create a feeling of welcome for our visitors. As a whole, our school should provide a safe, welcoming, and fun environment for our students to learn and grow.

Exercises Dialog Summary

Part 1 Dictation 🎧 30

Listen and fill in the blanks.

　Professor Terada and his students talk about the subject of elementary school planning and design. First, Professor Terada asks the students about the location of the school. Kimi thinks that school buildings should be built (　　　　　) apart from roads and streets, (　　　　) (　　　　　　) main traffic arteries. She feels that it would be effective both to reduce the possibility of dangerous accidents and to minimize traffic noise for classes. Victor thinks that it's better for schools to be built in (　　　　　) (　　　　　　) in order to have a lot of playground space and allow the students to have the opportunity to interact with nature. Serena (　　　　　) (　　　　　) (　　　　　) (　　　　　) (　　　　　) (　　　　　) it would be destructive to the environment because trees would need to be cleared. Professor Terada then asks about a situation in which they have to build a school building in a city close to busy roads and don't have much space.

Part 2 Dictation 🎧 31

Listen and fill in the blanks.

　Professor Terada and students have a (　　　　　　) about elementary school planning and design. Professor Terada begins by asking about the school's location. Kimi thinks school buildings should be built a (　　　　　) (　　　　　) from roads and streets. In her view, this would help both to reduce the possibility of dangerous accidents and to minimize traffic noise for classes. Victor thinks that building in suburban areas would increase the amount of playground space and (　　　　) (　　　　　) (　　　　　) (　　　　　　) have the opportunity to interact with nature. Serena notes that it would be destructive to the environment because trees would have to be cleared. Professor Terada proceeds to ask about a situation in which they have to build a school building in a city near busy roads and don't have much space. Kimi says that they need solid walls to (　　　　　) (　　　　　) and (　　　　　) (　　　　　) the local environment, including the ability to withstand strong storms. Victor thinks that the school's interior and grounds should be kept well lit at all times so that (　　　　　) (　　　　　) (　　　　　) (　　　　　) (　　　　　) (　　　　　　). Serena says that plants would protect children from (　　　　　) (　　　　　　). Victor agrees with her idea and suggests that they use flowers, which in his view would help to create a comfortable atmosphere. Kimi supports his idea, and feels that flowers near the entrance of the school would really help to (　　　　　) (　　　　　) (　　　　　) (　　　　　　) (　　　　　) (　　　　　) (　　　　　) (　　　　　　).

64

Part 3 Writing a summary

Answer the following questions and then write a summary of the dialog.

1. What do Professor Terada and the students discuss?
   _____

2. What is the first question Professor Terada asks?
   _____

3. What is the second question Professor Terada asks?
   _____

Grammar Focus — Verb Forms (3) and If-Clauses

> Both verbs with -ing forms and past participles can be used like adjectives or adverbs. An if-clause may be used to describe a certain condition: if something happens, then something else will happen. The subjunctive can also be used for hypothetical situations. In a short if-clause, the subject and verb "be" can sometimes be omitted.

Complete each of the following sentences with an appropriate word or phrase.

1. The participants in the (   ) experiment were happy when the research was completed.
   a. was exhausted   b. exhausting   c. exhausted   d. will be exhausted

2. He struggled to impress the (   ) audience with his presentation.
   a. distract   b. was distracting   c. was distracted   d. distracted

3. (   ) by buzzing mosquitoes, the campers stayed awake all through the night.
   a. Annoys   b. To annoy   c. Annoying   d. Annoyed

4. (   ) your telephone number, they would have called you earlier.
   a. If they know   b. They had known   c. If they had known   d. Have had known

5. (   ) the liquid starts to evaporate, this is an indication that the boiling point has been reached.
   a. of   b. if   c. for   d. but

6. Improvement of infrastructure such as refrigeration systems and reliable transport networks is needed in some (   ) countries.
   a. develop   b. develops   c. developing   d. will develop

7. What would you do if you (　　) awarded a valuable patent and could therefore retire?
   a. are　　　　　　b. was　　　　　　c. were　　　　　　d. had

8. I'm going to the Bionanoelectronics Center and I'll tell you if I (　　) your graph paper there.
   a. find　　　　　　b. finding　　　　c. found　　　　　d. had found

9. (　　) you forget your password?
   a. Of　　　　　　　b. If but　　　　　c. What if　　　　　d. Just

10. After reading the computer manual, feel free to contact us (　　).
    a. if necessary　　b. if any　　　　　c. if will need　　　d. if doubt

Writing Assignments　Writing a Persuasive Paragraph

A Ask your partner about the most impressive building he or she has ever seen, and why.

B Write a short paragraph about the building discussed in **A** above.

C Write a paragraph about the most impressive building you've ever seen. Use details and reasons to support your response.

Unit 11 Art and Science

Quick Survey Ask the following five questions to your partner. Then, write your answers, your partner's answers, and the most popular answers in your group or class.

Question	Your answer	Your partner's answer	Most popular answer
1. Do you use a tablet computer?			
2. What is your opinion of tablet computers?			
3. Do you think that advanced technology can be dangerous?			
4. What kinds of movies do you like?			
5. Do you think that movies can influence science? How?			

Dialog 32

Taro is reading an online newspaper article using a tablet computer.

Serena: Is a tablet more convenient than a laptop computer?

Taro: Yeah, they're a lot more convenient. They are really light, and good enough for reading books and articles.

Serena: I like stylish new devices like the tablet computer.

5 Taro: Actually, it's not a very new idea. The iPad was the first one to become popular, but in fact there have been other tablet computers in the past.

Serena: Wow, really? I had no clue.

Taro: Yep. In fact, before they were even invented, tablet-like computers were often seen in popular science fiction TV programs and movies. For example, actors in the TV show
10   *Star Trek* used devices that looked like tablet computers. In the excellent Stanley Kubrick movie *2001: A Space Odyssey,* a computer is used which looks and functions

	exactly like an iPad. The movie is from 1968! It was co-written by Kubrick and the British science fiction writer Arthur C. Clarke.
Serena:	Actually, I've also seen a few Kubrick movies. Besides *2001*, I really love *Dr. Strangelove*, for example. I feel that Kubrick's genius is his eye; the way his films look. His cinematography is absolutely unique, and no one else can make a film that looks like his films. From his use of color, images, different camera angles, and music, we know that Kubrick has an extremely unique perspective. Seeing most of his movies is like looking around inside the mind of a genius. So it doesn't surprise me that something similar to a tablet computer appeared in one of his movies so long ago.
Taro:	That's a good point, and it doesn't surprise me, either. Kubrick's movies are well known for their impact on society, including themes such as the ways in which science and technology can influence the course of humanity. In *2001: A Space Odyssey*, for example, one of the main characters is a computer called "HAL." HAL is a computer that tries to hurt people. These days, HAL is used as a kind of example of what can go wrong with artificial intelligence. *Dr. Strangelove* explores a similar idea: the danger inherent in the computer control of nuclear weapons.
Serena:	Based on what you're saying, it seems that Kubrick was a visionary, not unlike many famous scientists.
Taro:	Indeed. You know, people say "life imitates art." That's true, and I think "science imitates art" is also true. Even if they do not intentionally mean to collaborate, I feel that scientists and artists inspire each other through their creative endeavors to push society forward.
Serena:	That sounds reasonable to me.

Exercises Dialog Summary

Part 1 Dictation 🎧 33

Listen and fill in the blanks.

Taro is using a tablet computer, and (　　　　) that it's light and more (　　　　) for reading books and articles than a laptop computer. He tells Serena that tablet-like computers can be viewed in science fiction TV programs and movies such as *Star Trek* and *2001: A Space Odyssey*. Serena has also seen a few Kubrick movies, and she thinks he has an extremely (　　　　) (　　　　). She feels that seeing his movies is like looking around inside (　　　　) (　　　　) (　　　　) (　　　　) (　　　　). Taro talks about the movie *2001: A Space Odyssey* and its main character, called "HAL." HAL is a computer that tries to hurt people, and today this film is used to (　　　　) (　　　　) (　　　　) (　　　　) (　　　　) (　　　　) (　　　　) of artificial intelligence. *Dr. Strangelove* is another Kubrick movie, and it (　　　　) (　　　　) a similar idea: the danger (　　　　) (　　　　) the computer control of nuclear weapons.

Part 2 Dictation 🎧 34

Listen and fill in the blanks.

Taro uses a tablet computer, and states that it's light and more convenient for reading books and articles than a laptop computer. He says that tablet-like computers appear in popular science fiction TV programs and movies like *Star Trek* and *2001: A Space Odyssey*. Serena has also seen a few Kubrick movies. She feels that he has an extremely unique perspective, and viewing his movies is similar to looking around inside the mind of a genius. Taro discusses the movie *2001: A Space Odyssey* and its main character, a computer named "HAL." HAL tries to (　　　　) people, and these days it's used as a kind of example of problems that can (　　　　) from the use of artificial intelligence. *Dr. Strangelove* is also a Kubrick movie, and it explores the idea that there is danger inherent in the computer control of nuclear weapons. Serena says that Kubrick was (　　　　) a visionary, and had (　　　　) (　　　　) many famous scientists. Taro (　　　　) that scientists and artists inspire each other through their creative endeavors to push society forward.

Part 3 Writing a summary

Answer the following questions and then write a summary of the dialog.

1. What do Taro and Serena say about Stanley Kubrick movies?

_____

2. What is HAL?

3. What does Taro mean when he says that "science imitates art"?

Grammar Focus — Adjective Clauses—Relative Clauses

Adjective clauses may also be called relative clauses. They can be used to connect two sentences. The appropriate selection of a relative pronoun depends on what word it refers to and where the word is placed in the second sentence.

Complete each of the following sentences with an appropriate word or phrase.

1. This kind of research is vital to (   ) study and value the environment, nature, and animals in the wild.
   a. who   **b.** whose   **c.** whom   **d.** those who

2. They say that there are a lot of people in Asia and Africa (   ) eat insects as part of their regular diet.
   a. who   **b.** whose   **c.** whom   **d.** those who

3. It is a non-profit organization (   ) purpose is to improve the lives of deprived children.
   a. who   **b.** whose   **c.** which   **d.** of which

4. You can search job openings (   ) may include modern health care, hospitals, pharmaceuticals, and so on.
   a. which   **b.** that which   **c.** who   **d.** whom

5. The old ship was covered in coral, (   ) made it difficult to see from a distance.
   a. what   **b.** which   **c.** whom   **d.** that which

6. One of the professors is looking for a student (   ) to do research.
   a. who   **b.** whom   **c.** with whom   **d.** whose

7. Physics is a science (   ) involves matter and energy, and a wide variety of systems as well, (   ) theories have been developed that are used by physicists.
   a. which, which   **b.** which, on which   **c.** that, of which   **d.** that, about which

8. The cell phone salesperson was very surprised when he visited a remote village (　　　) locals had never owned cell phones.
   a. in which　　　b. of which　　　c. at which　　　d. both of which

9. In the Devonian period, jawed fishes included the placoderms and spiny sharks, (　　　) became extinct.
   a. in which　　　b. of which　　　c. at which　　　d. both of which

10. The characteristics of igneous rocks are defined by the size and shape of the grains (　　　) they are composed.
    a. in which　　　b. of which　　　c. at which　　　d. both of which

Writing Assignments — Writing an Argumentative Paragraph

A Ask your partner whether he or she is more in agreement with the statement "life imitates art" or "science imitates art", and why.

Art and Science

B Write a short paragraph regarding the expressions "life imitates art" and "science imitates art," based on your partner's response in **A** above.

C Write a paragraph about whether you are more in agreement with the statement "life imitates art" or "science imitates art," and explain why.

Unit 12 The Structure of the Universe (1)

Quick Survey

Ask the following five questions to your partner. Then, write your answers, your partner's answers, and the most popular answers in your group or class.

Question	Your answer	Your partner's answer	Most popular answer
1. Do you like to gaze at stars at night?			
2. Have you ever been to a planetarium?			
3. How many stars can you name, in English?			
4. Can you tell me their names, and anything you know about them?			
5. Would you like to travel into space?			

Lecture   35

Professor Brown lectures his students about the structure of the universe. He thinks that if people have a deeper understanding of the universe, it can improve their lives. He hopes that some students will be motivated to do further research on this topic outside of class.

Prof. Brown:

1 Good morning, students. Today, we'll talk about the structure of the universe, and our location in it. You probably think you know where you are right now. But do you... really? We look up at the sky at night and see many little points of light, but they
5 are very far away and therefore they are difficult to see clearly and identify. With a telescope, we can view some of them in considerable detail. For example, here's a photo I took of Jupiter, using a telescope.

Jupiter

The Structure of the Universe (1)

2 Here's a photo of Saturn, taken using the same telescope. It's not nearly as detailed as a Hubble image, but anyway I like it! Saturn is kind of cute.

Saturn

3 So, let's begin. As I said, when we look at the sky at night without a telescope, we see most stars, planets, and other objects in space as mere points of light. We can't see any detail, they mostly just look like white dots. So, we say that the stars are pretty, and forget about them. Space seems almost abstract to us. We feel like space is "up there" and "far away"... and we live on earth, a place separate from space. However, this is incorrect. Earth is part of space. We live in space, we are a part of space. In fact, most of the elements in our bodies were created inside stars.

4 You probably know the names of your street, town, prefecture, country, and continent: your location on earth. In fact, when you don't know your location, you feel disoriented. Being disoriented is a very uncomfortable and confusing feeling. So, most people like to know where they are.

5 However, knowing our address on earth is only a very small part of knowing our true location. We are like goldfish in a tank called "earth," and the earth is but a tiny speck in an unimaginably large universe. If we only know our location on earth and not in the universe, it's like we are goldfish who don't know what's outside our tank—or even where the tank is! Perhaps many people often feel a bit disoriented because they don't have any idea where they actually are, so the universe seems confusing and mysterious. Therefore, isn't it a good idea to learn about the structure of the universe, and our exact location inside it? Once we learn these things, perhaps life and existence will feel less disorienting, and more comfortable. There is really no reason for "the universe," and our location in it, to be a mystery. It's quite easy to understand.

Exercises   Comprehension

Part 1

Question   Read and listen to the 1st and 2nd paragraphs, and answer the following questions.

1. What is the topic of the lecture?

2. What do we see when we look up at the sky at night?

3. How does the use of a telescope change the view?

4. What objects are visible in the professor's two photographs?

Discussion   Read and listen to the 1st and 2nd paragraphs again, and discuss the story with your partner using the following key phrases.

- the structure of the universe
- our location
- you know where you are
- the sky at night
- many little points of light
- far away
- difficult to see
- with a telescope
- considerable detail
- a photo of Jupiter
- a photo of Saturn
- not nearly as detailed as a Hubble image

Dictation   Listen and fill in the blanks.   🎧 36

Professor Brown gives a lecture on (　　　　)(　　　　)(　　　　)
(　　　　)(　　　　)(　　　　)(　　　　)(　　　　)
(　　　　)(　　　　). He suspects that many people don't actually know where they are. He says that when we look up at the sky at night, (　　　　)(　　　　)(　　　　)
(　　　　)(　　　　)(　　　　)(　　　　). However, with a telescope, we can see objects in space (　　　　)(　　　　)(　　　　)
(　　　　). Professor Brown shares (　　　　)(　　　　)(　　　　)
(　　　　)(　　　　)(　　　　) using a telescope. He likes his photos even though they do not rival the quality of pictures taken using the Hubble Space Telescope.

Part 2

Question Read and listen to the 3rd and 4th paragraphs, and answer the following questions.

1. Without a telescope, what do we see as mere points of light?
   _____

2. According to Professor Brown, how do people feel about space?
   _____

3. What is our relationship with space?
   _____

4. Where were most of the elements in our bodies created?
   _____

5. Why do most people like to know where they are?
   _____

Discussion Read and listen to the 3rd and 4th paragraphs again, and discuss the story with your partner using the following key words and phrases.

3rd Paragraph

- without a telescope
- stars, planets
- other objects in space
- points of light
- pretty
- forget about them
- abstract
- up there
- far away
- live on earth
- separate from space
- incorrect
- earth
- part of space
- live in space
- the elements in our bodies
- inside stars

4th Paragraph

- your street, town, prefecture, country, and continent
- location on earth
- when you don't know your location
- you feel disoriented
- uncomfortable and confusing
- people like to know where they are

Dictation Listen and fill in the blanks. 🎧 37

Professor Brown says that we don't pay much attention to objects in space because they appear quite small without a telescope, and thus (   ) (   ) (   ). We feel that the earth is separate from space. Space seems (   ) (   ). Professor Brown says that (   ) (   ) (   ) (   ) (   ) because the earth is part of space. Most of the elements in our bodies were created (   ) (   ). The professor also says that most people like to know where they are (   ) (   ) (   ) (   ) (   ) because the feeling is actually very (   ) (   ) (   ).

Part 3

Question Read and listen to the 5th paragraph, and answer the following questions.

1. Can you explain Professor Brown's analogy which refers to "goldfish"?
   _____

2. According to the lecture, why do many people often feel disoriented?
   _____

3. What does the professor feel is a good idea to learn about?
   _____

Discussion Read and listen to the 5th paragraph again, and discuss the story with your partner using the following key phrases.

- our address on earth
- goldfish in a tank
- the earth is a tiny speck
- don't know what's outside our tank
- where the tank is
- don't have any idea where they actually are
- the universe
- confusing and mysterious
- the structure of the universe
- our exact location
- life and existence
- less disorienting and more comfortable
- no reason for the universe to be a mystery
- our location
- easy to understand

78

The Structure of the Universe (1)

Dictation Listen and fill in the blanks. 🎧 38

Professor Brown says that our situation is analogous to that of ( ) ( ) ( ) ( ) ( ). By learning where our location is in the universe, ( ) ( ) ( ) ( ) ( ) ( ) ( ) ( ). Although the universe seems confusing and mysterious, it's a good idea to learn about ( ) ( ) ( ) ( ) ( ) ( ) ( ) ( ), so life and existence will feel less disorienting and more comfortable.

Writing Assignments — Writing a Summary Paragraph (1)

Write a paragraph summarizing the lecture which includes the following key phrases.

- ▶ the structure of the universe
- ▶ stars, planets, and other objects in space
- ▶ part of space
- ▶ our location on earth
- ▶ feel disoriented
- ▶ confusing and mysterious

Unit 13 The Structure of the Universe (2)

Lecture 39

Professor Brown continues his lecture on the structure of the universe. He decides to start by discussing the Earth. The professor straightens his tie, and readies presentation software on a notebook computer.

Prof. Brown:

1 So, let's talk about... our location! Where are we, exactly? Well, of course, we are in Japan. Japan is on the planet Earth.

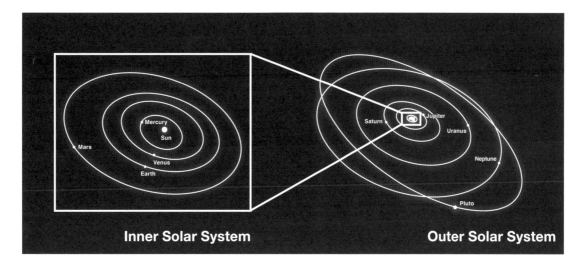

2 Earth is in the solar system. The solar system consists of the Earth, other planets, moons, and various other objects which revolve around the sun. Let's take a trip! If we travel into space, away from the Earth, we can take a look behind us and see the inner solar system.

3 As we continue to travel, we look back again, and now we can see the entire (both the inner and outer) solar system. The inner planets are much closer to the sun, and much closer to each other, than the outer planets.

4 Our solar system is not close to anything else, so as we move further away from it, we see mostly empty space. We are very small, and very alone.

5 As we move even further away from our solar system, we can finally view some other star systems. The star which is closest to Earth is called Proxima Centauri. It is part of Alpha Centauri, a system of three stars which are near each other. However, these stars are only visible from the southern hemisphere of the Earth. The closest, and brightest star we can see from our location in Japan is called Sirius.

6 Alpha Centauri is 4.37 light years away. It would take the Space Shuttle approximately 165,000 years to travel to these stars, our closest neighbors. Scientists believe that there may be planets in the Alpha Centauri star system which harbor life, but it's impossible to go and investigate. Sometimes, people say that they don't believe that aliens exist because if there were really aliens, they would visit us. But in reality, there could easily be millions, even billions of different types of creatures living all over the universe. The problem is distance; we definitely can't get to them, and they probably can't get to us.

Exercises Comprehension

Part 1

Question Read and listen to the 1st and 2nd paragraphs, and answer the following questions.

1. Which location does Professor Brown discuss at the beginning of his lecture?
   _____

2. How does Professor Brown describe the solar system?
   _____

3. According to Professor Brown, what can we see if we travel into space and look behind us?
   _____

Discussion Read and listen to the 1st and 2nd paragraphs again, and discuss the story with your partner using the following key words and phrases.

- Japan
- on the planet Earth
- the solar system
- other planets, moons, and various other objects
- revolve around the sun
- travel into space
- the inner solar system

Dictation Listen and fill in the blanks. 🎧 40

   Professor Brown describes ( ) ( ), using presentation software for assistance. He begins with Japan, then moves on to the planet Earth. ( ) ( ) ( ) consists of the Earth, other planets, moons, and various other objects ( ) ( ) ( ) ( ) ( ). The class takes a virtual trip into space. If they turn around and look behind them near the beginning of the trip, they can see ( ) ( ) ( ) ( ).

82

The Structure of the Universe (2)

Part 2

Question Read and listen to the 3rd and 4th paragraphs, and answer the following questions.

1. As the students continue their imaginary trip and look back, what can they see?
   _____

2. What are two differences between the inner and outer planets?
   _____

3. How might we feel if we saw the empty space surrounding our solar system?
   _____

Discussion Read and listen to the 3rd and 4th paragraphs again, and discuss the story with your partner using the following key phrases.

- ▶ the entire (both the inner and outer) solar system
- ▶ much closer to the sun
- ▶ much closer to each other
- ▶ empty space
- ▶ very small and very alone

Dictation Listen and fill in the blanks. 🎧 41

   Professor Brown and students continue their imaginary trip, and they see (　　　　　) (　　　　　) (　　　　　) (　　　　　). (　　　　　) (　　　　　) (　　　　　) are much closer to the sun and one another (　　　　　) (　　　　　) (　　　　　) (　　　　　). The professor comments that as our solar system is really not close to anything else, we feel (　　　　　) (　　　　　) (　　　　　) (　　　　　) (　　　　　), (　　　　　) (　　　　　) (　　　　　) when we see mostly empty space.

Part 3

Question Read and listen to the 5th and 6th paragraphs, and answer the following questions.

1. Which star is closest to Earth?
   _____

2. From which location can we view Alpha Centauri?
   _____

3. How far away is Alpha Centauri?

_____

4. How long would it take to travel to Alpha Centauri from our planet?

_____

5. Why can't we confirm if there is life in other parts of the universe?

_____

Discussion Read and listen to the 5th and 6th paragraphs again, and discuss the story with your partner using the following key phrases.

- move further away from our solar system
- Proxima Centauri
- Alpha Centauri
- a system of three stars
- only visible from the southern hemisphere
- 4.37 light years away
- take the Space Shuttle
- approximately 165,000 years
- scientists believe
- harbor life
- impossible to go there and investigate
- don't believe that aliens exist
- millions, even billions of different types of creatures living
- the problem is distance

Dictation Listen and fill in the blanks. 🎧 42

The students can finally view (　　　　　) (　　　　　), a system of three stars. The closest star to Earth is (　　　　　) (　　　　　) (　　　　　). Alpha Centauri is only visible from the southern hemisphere of the Earth. It is (　　　　　) (　　　　　) (　　　　　) away, and it would take the Space Shuttle (　　　　　) (　　　　　) (　　　　　) to travel to these stars. Scientists believe that there could be planets in the Alpha Centauri star system which harbor life, but (　　　　　) (　　　　　) (　　　　　) (　　　　　) (　　　　　) (　　　　　), so we can't confirm it. Some people don't believe that aliens exist, but there could be billions of various kinds of creatures living all over the universe.

The Structure of the Universe (2)

Writing Assignments — Writing a Summary Paragraph (2)

Write a paragraph summarizing the lecture which includes the following key phrases.

- on the planet Earth
- the solar system
- travel into space
- the inner solar system
- the outer solar system
- move further away from our solar system
- Proxima Centauri
- Alpha Centauri
- harbor life
- aliens exist

Unit 14 The Structure of the Universe (3)

Lecture 43

> Professor Brown continues his lecture and concludes by discussing superclusters. He thinks that it is important to do this so the students can have a comprehensive understanding of the structure of the universe.

Prof. Brown:

1 So, we are continuing to travel further away from the Earth. Now, many more millions of stars come into our view. Our solar system is located in the Local Arm of the Milky Way Galaxy.

2 Let's travel even further away from our solar system. We can now see the entire Milky Way. Do you see the label "Sun" in the picture below? That's our exact location, in the Local Arm (also called the Orion Arm) of the Milky Way. We can also see the Galactic Bulge at the center of our galaxy. The Galactic Bulge (also called the Galactic Center) of our galaxy is a mysterious and amazing place. It is thought that at its center is a massive black hole. There are many stars in the Galactic Bulge: it has the highest density of stars in the galaxy. In the entire Milky Way, there are thought to be about 300,000,000,000 stars.

3 Everything in the Milky Way orbits *(revolves around)* the Galactic Bulge. It takes about 220,000,000 years for us to complete one revolution around it. That's a really long time, so the sun and Earth have completed less than 25 orbits around the Galactic Bulge since they formed.

4 As we move further away, a few other much smaller galaxies come into view. For example, the Large Magellanic Cloud and the Small Magellanic Cloud are both neighbors of the Milky Way.

5 Next, we can see that we are part of a group of more than 30 galaxies called the Local Group. The largest of these is called the Andromeda Galaxy. Andromeda is similar in size and shape to the Milky Way. It is believed that in the future, the Milky Way and Andromeda will move together and combine to form a huge new spiral galaxy. If you want to travel to Andromeda using a spacecraft like the Space Shuttle, you should bring a lot of food because it will take you more than 80,000,000,000 years to get there.

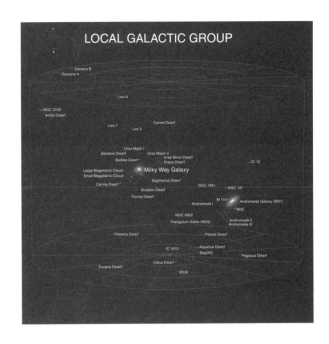

6 As we continue to travel away from the Earth, things really start to become strange. The Local Group, our home, is actually part of a much larger group of galaxies called the Virgo Supercluster. A supercluster is a large group of smaller galaxy groups. There are more than 5,000 galaxies in the Virgo Supercluster, and the volume of the Virgo Supercluster is about 100,000,000,000 times that of the Milky Way! It has recently been discovered that the Virgo Supercluster is part of an even bigger supercluster called the Laniakea Supercluster. Amazingly, there are millions of superclusters in the universe.

7 It is believed that there are around 10,000,000 superclusters of galaxies in the universe, which would mean that there are more than 100,000,000,000 galaxies in total. So, the entire universe is believed to look like this shocking picture: millions of superclusters of galaxies.

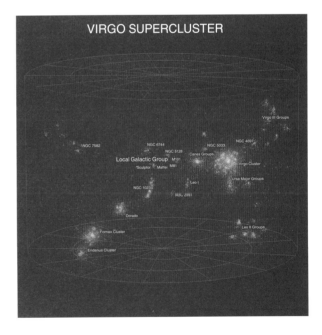

Exercises Comprehension

Part 1

Question   Read and listen to the 1st, 2nd and 3rd paragraphs, and answer the following questions.

1. Where is our solar system located?

   _____

2. What is at the center of our galaxy?

   _____

3. What is at the center of the Galactic Bulge?

   _____

4. How many stars are in the Milky Way?

   _____

5. How many years does it take for the Earth to complete one revolution around the Galactic Bulge?

   _____

Discussion   Read and listen to the 1st, 2nd and 3rd paragraphs again, and discuss the story with your partner using the following key phrases.

- ▶ continuing to travel further away
- ▶ many more millions of stars
- ▶ the Local Arm of the Milky Way Galaxy
- ▶ the Galactic Bulge
- ▶ a mysterious and amazing place
- ▶ a massive black hole
- ▶ the highest density of stars in the galaxy
- ▶ 300,000,000,000 stars
- ▶ everything in the Milky Way
- ▶ about 220,000,000 years
- ▶ one revolution around it
- ▶ less than 25 orbits

Dictation   Listen and fill in the blanks.   44

Professor Brown and his students continue their imaginary journey away from the Earth. The professor says that our solar system is situated in (　　　　　) (　　　　　) (　　　　　) (　　　　　) (　　　　　) (　　　　　) (　　　　　). At the center of our galaxy is (　　　　　) (　　　　　) (　　　　　).

The Structure of the Universe (3)

It is a mysterious and amazing place because it is believed that there is (   )
(   ) (   ) (   ) at its center, and it has (   )
(   ) (   ) (   ) (   ) in the galaxy. It is thought
that there are (   ) (   ) (   ) in the entire Milky Way.
Everything in the Milky Way orbits around the Galactic Bulge. It takes about 220,000,000 years for us to complete a single revolution around it, and it is believed that the sun and the earth have completed less than 25 orbits since they formed.

Part 2

Question Read and listen to the 4th and 5th paragraphs, and answer the following questions.

1. As the virtual trip continues, what much smaller galaxies can the class see?
   _____

2. What is the name of our group of more than 30 galaxies?
   _____

3. What is the largest galaxy in the group called?
   _____

4. In theory, what will happen to Milky Way and Andromeda in the future?
   _____

5. How many years would it take to go to Andromeda by spacecraft?
   _____

Discussion Read and listen to the 4th and 5th paragraphs again, and discuss the story with your partner using the following key phrases.

- much smaller galaxies
- the Large Magellanic Cloud
- the Small Magellanic Cloud
- neighbors of the Milky Way
- a group of more than 30 galaxies
- the Local Group
- the Andromeda Galaxy

- similar in size and shape to the Milky Way
- the Milky Way and Andromeda
- will move together
- combine to form a huge new spiral galaxy
- using a spacecraft like the Space Shuttle
- more than 80,000,000,000 years

Unit 14

Dictation   Listen and fill in the blanks. 🎧 45

　　Professor Brown and his students move further away from home, and can now see (　　　　) (　　　　) (　　　　) (　　　　) (　　　　) (　　　　), including the Large Magellanic Cloud and the Small Magellanic Cloud. These smaller galaxies are next to the Milky Way. Next, they can see our group of more than 30 galaxies, called (　　　　) (　　　　) (　　　　). The largest one is called the Andromeda Galaxy, which is (　　　　) (　　　　) (　　　　) (　　　　) (　　　　) (　　　　) (　　　　) (　　　　) (　　　　). The Milky Way and Andromeda will theoretically move together and combine (　　　　) (　　　　) (　　　　) (　　　　) (　　　　) (　　　　) (　　　　) in the future. Using a spacecraft like the Space Shuttle, it would take (　　　　) (　　　　) (　　　　) (　　　　) to travel to Andromeda.

Part 3

Question   Read and listen to the 6th and 7th paragraphs, and answer the following questions.

1. What much larger group of galaxies can they see?

   _____

2. How many galaxies does the Virgo Supercluster contain?

   _____

3. What is the volume of the Virgo Supercluster compared to the Milky Way?

   _____

4. According to the professor, approximately how many galaxies are there in the universe?

   _____

Discussion   Read and listen to the 6th and 7th paragraphs again, and discuss the story with your partner using the following key phrases.

▶ a much larger group of galaxies
▶ the Virgo Supercluster
▶ a large group of smaller galaxy groups
▶ more than 5,000 galaxies
▶ about 100,000,000,000 times
▶ Laniakea Supercluster

▶ around 10,000,000 superclusters of galaxies in the universe
▶ more than 100,000,000,000 galaxies in total
▶ millions of superclusters of galaxies

The Structure of the Universe (3)

Dictation Listen and fill in the blanks. 🎧 46

Professor Brown and his students continue to travel further away, and they can see the Local Group, which is part of a much larger group of galaxies called (   ) (   ) (   ). The Virgo Supercluster is a large group of smaller galaxy groups and includes (   ) (   ) (   ) (   ). Its volume is (   ) (   ) (   ) that of the Milky Way. According to a recent report, the Virgo Supercluster is part of an even bigger supercluster called the Laniakea Supercluster. There are reportedly around 10,000,000 superclusters of galaxies in the universe, which would mean that there are (   ) (   ) (   ) (   ) in total. The professor remarks that the entire universe consists of millions of superclusters of galaxies.

Writing Assignments — Writing a Summary Paragraph (3)

Write a paragraph summarizing the lecture which includes the following key phrases.

- the Local Arm of the Milky Way Galaxy
- the Galactic Bulge
- a massive black hole
- the highest density of stars in the galaxy
- the Large Magellanic Cloud and the Small Magellanic Cloud
- the Local Group
- the Andromeda Galaxy
- the Milky Way and Andromeda
- the Virgo Supercluster
- more than 100,000,000,000 galaxies in total

Example of a Future Resume

Shun Sugiyama

School Address:
5-5, Manabu
Higashi-ku, Tokyo 140-0909
Japan

Permanent Address:
123 Akarui Street
Kawagoe-shi, Saitama 366-0040
Japan
+81-049-239-0300
sugishun@tkypacific.ac.jp

Objective	Seeking an entry-level position with a manufacturer of precision instruments, measuring instruments, and medical equipment
Education	Tokyo Pacific University, 5-5, Manabu, Higashi-ku, Tokyo 140-0909 Bachelor of Science and Engineering Anticipated Graduation: March 20XX Atoboshi High School, Sugamo, Tokyo Graduation: March 20XX
Experience	*Intern*, JAXA Sagamihara Campus (Summer 20XX) – Volunteered 35 hours per week – Collected data and created a database of information, charts and graphs using Microsoft Excel – Wrote numerous articles based upon interviews with graduate students and lab assistants *Exchange Student*, Hubble University, New York (August 22, 20XX–May 15, 20XX) *Vice-President*, Science Club (Spring 20XX to present) *Assistant*, Academic Enhancement Center (20XX–20XX) *Teaching Assistant*, Chemistry Lab (Fall 20XX) *Assistant*, Advanced Science and Technology Lab, summer camp for high school students (Summer 20XX)
Activities/ Honors	Participated in English Language Training Program for Science and Engineering Students at Hubble University, New York (March 20XX) Awarded 1st Prize, Science Intercollege Competition, Ministry of Education, Culture, Sports, Science and Technology (February 20XX) Volunteered for wildlife conservation projects in Africa (Summer 20XX)
Skills	Native Japanese, intermediate English, TOEIC L&R: 900 (20XX) Microsoft Office (Access, Excel, Publisher, PowerPoint, Word) Programming: C/C++, BASIC, HTML Certificate, Information Technology Passport Examination Certificate, Examination for Biomedical Engineering (Class 2) Teacher's License for Mathematics, Science, and Industrial Technology: Junior High School, High School

未来の英文履歴書の例

杉山　駿

大学所在地： 140-0909 東京都東区学5-5	現住所： 366-0040 埼玉県川越市 赤頬町123 81-049-239-0300 sugishun@tkypacific.ac.jp

希望職種	大卒レベル　精密機械、計測器、医療機器の製造
学歴	20XX年3月　東京太平洋大学（140-0909 東京都東区学5-5） 理工学科卒業見込み　理工学学士取得予定 20XX年3月　後星高校（東京都巣鴨）卒業
職歴	20XX年夏期　インターンシップ　JAXA相模原キャンパス ・週35時間のボランティア活動 ・エクセルを使ったデータ集計及びデータベース作成 ・大学院生及び実験助手へのインタビューに基づいた記事を多数執筆 20XX年8月22日〜20XX年5月15日　ハッブル大学（ニューヨーク市）交換留学派遣生 20XX年春学期〜現在　サイエンスクラブ副部長 20XX〜20XX年　学習支援センター補助員 20XX年秋学期　化学実験教育補助員 20XX年夏期　高校生のための夏季プログラム：先進的科学技術実験体験授業補助員
活動・賞罰	20XX年3月　理工学部英語研修プログラム参加（ニューヨーク市・ハッブル大学） 20XX年2月　文部科学省主催サイエンスインカレ優勝 20XX年夏期　アフリカ野生生物保護プロジェクトボランティア参加
特技・資格	母語：日本語、英語：中級レベル、TOEIC L&R：900点（20XX年受験） マイクロソフトオフィス（アクセス、エクセル、パブリッシャー、パワーポイント、ワード） プログラミング（C/C++、BASIC、HTML） ITパスポート取得 第2種ME技術者※ 中学校・高等学校教諭1種免許状（数学、理科、工業）

※「ME機器・システムの安全管理を中心とした医用生体工学に関する知識をもち、適切な指導のもとで、それを実際に医療に応用しうる資質」を検定する試験。

Glossary

Unit 1

good at ...	…が得意な
Can I have your name?	「名前を教えてください」
background	経歴
medical device	医療機器
achieve	（目標など）…を達成する、実現する
objective (*n*)	目的、目標
tough question	難しい質問
attain	（目標など）…を達成する、実現する
goal	目的、目標
I still don't get it.	「まだ理解できない（納得できない）」
elaborate	…を詳しく説明する
personal history	履歴、経歴、自分史
attend	（学校など）…に行く、出席する、参加する
You bet!	「その通りです」「おっしゃる通りです」
strength	強み、長所
weakness	欠点、短所
vice versa	逆もまた同様
objective (*adj*)	客観的な
profile	（人物などについて）…の概略を書く
mount	マウント、望遠鏡架台　※望遠鏡の鏡筒部を支えて固定する機械構造物
enclosure	エンクロージャー　※大型望遠鏡を格納する筒型の建物
observatory	天文台、気象台

Unit 2

journal	日誌、日記
civil engineering	土木工学
provisional	仮の、臨時の
set a goal	目標を定める
practice	練習
investigate	…を調査する
field	領域、分野
focus on ...	…に重点的に取り組む、…に集中する
accomplish	（目標など）…を達成する、実現する
career	職業の、キャリアの
outline	…の概要をまとめる
long term	長期間
make use of ...	…を活用する
talent	才能、素質
comprehensively	総合的に、包括的に
That makes sense.	「それなら納得できます」
summarize	（話など）…を要約する、簡単にまとめる
review	…を再検討する
semester	（1年が2学期制の）学期
Sounds like a plan.	「よい考えですね」
job hunting	就職活動
safety equipment	安全装置
full-body exercise	全身運動
skeletal system	骨格系
solar eclipse	日食
chemical burns	化学火傷、化学的熱傷
ethics committee	倫理委員会

Unit 3

librarian	図書館員、司書
Time magazine	『タイム』誌　※米国のニュース週刊誌
view	…を見る
appropriate	（…に）適した
recommend	…を推薦する
audiovisual	視聴覚の
Chemical Abstracts	化学および関連分野の文献抄録誌　※現在はデータベース化されている
get access to ...	…を利用する
safeguard	…を保護する
prevent	…を防止する
unauthorized removal of ...	…を無断で持ち出すこと
check out ...	…を借り出す、貸し出す
self-checkout machine	自動貸出機

wriggle	うごめく、くねくね動く

Unit 4

ordinary	普通の
electronic device	電子装置
amazing	驚くべき、すばらしい
invention	発明
Edison	トーマス・エジソン　※米国の発明家（1847-1931）
phonograph	蓄音機
inventor	発明家
incredible	信じられない、すばらしい
unbelievable	信じられない、すばらしい
electric light bulb	白熱電球
electric power generation and distribution	発電と配電
kinetoscope	活動写真映写機
website	ウェブサイト、ホームページ
Library of Congress	米国議会図書館
extraordinary	並はずれた、非常な
sulfur	硫黄
humpback whale	ザトウクジラ
extinct	絶滅した
endangered	絶滅の危機にひんした

Unit 5

gorgeous	すばらしい、見事な
telescope	望遠鏡
astrophotography	天体写真術
scope	telescope の略
overhead	頭上に
atmosphere	大気
proper	適切な
precaution	予防措置
Herschel wedge	ハーシェル・プリズム　※接眼レンズ系に取り付けて太陽光を分光するプリズム
sunspot	太陽の黒点
magnetic activity	磁気活動
coherent	可干渉性（波動の位相がそろっている状態）の
on board	（船や飛行機に）乗って
computer-controlled	コンピュータ制御の
algebra	代数学
equation	方程式
Tiger Swallowtail butterfly	トラフアゲハチョウ
blue whale	シロナガスクジラ

Unit 6

online	オンラインの、インターネット上の、ネットワーク上の
social networking service	SNS　※インターネットを通じて構築する社会的ネットワークを提供するサービス（LINE や Facebook、Twitter など）
text message	簡易電子メールを送る
avoid	…を避ける
addict	依存症、中毒者
addicted	中毒になっている
addictive	中毒になりやすい
admit	…を認める
instant messaging	インスタントメッセージ、簡易メッセージ
face-to-face communication	直接会って行うコミュニケーション
packet-switching network	パケット通信網
advent	出現、登場
general population	一般集団
spacecraft	宇宙船

Unit 7

run a company	会社を経営する
vacuum cleaner	電気掃除機
detect	…を発券する、検出する
obstacle	障害物
consumer electronics maker	家電メーカー
disaster site	被災地
take an active role	活躍する、積極的に取り組む
oil spill	石油流出　※海上で起こることを指す
docking station	接続架台　※ここでは充電するホームベースを指す
rechargeable battery	充電式電池
adapt	…を適合させる
people with disabilities	体に不自由がある人、障がい者
marketplace	市場
No question.	「疑いの余地がありません」「ごもっともです」
platelet	血小板
fatal disease	致命的疾患、不治の病
forensic science lab	犯罪化学研究所

adverse reaction	拒絶反応、副作用

Unit 8

conduct an experiment	実験をする
analyze	分析する、解析する
water pollution	水質汚染
water monitoring kit	水監視装置一式（セット）
test tube	試験管
plot	（グラフ上に点）…を書く、プロットする
coliform bacteria	大腸菌群
dissolved oxygen	溶存酸素（量）〔略はDO〕 ※水中に溶け込んでいる酸素
biochemical oxygen demand	生物化学的酸素要求量（BOD）
nitrate	硝酸塩
phosphate	リン酸塩
pH	ペーハー、水素（イオン）指数
suspended solids	浮遊物質、懸濁物（SS）
disturbing	気掛かりな
indication	指し示すもの
moderate	中程度の
normal range	正常範囲
turbidity	濁度、濁りの度合い
take part in ...	…に参加する
Hudson River	ハドソン川　※米国ニューヨーク州の川
PCB	ポリ塩化ビフェニル〔polychlorinated biphenylの略〕
contamination	汚染
ban	…を禁止する
advocate	擁護者、支持者
cleanup campaign	清掃運動
vary depending on ...	…によって変わる
proceed with ...	…を進める、実行する
dormitory	寮
academic conference	学会

Unit 9

optical illusions	錯視（視覚における錯覚、目の錯覚）
have good eyesight	視力が良い
notice	…に気が付く
imperfection	欠陥、欠点、不完全
fool	だます、欺く　▶ be fooled by ...「…にだまされる」
perceive	…を知覚する
appear	（…のように）見える、思える
bend	曲がる
straight	まっすぐな
perfectly	完全に
still	静止している、動かない
remind A of B	AにBを思い出させる、連想させる
vase	花びん
stare at ...	…をじっと見つめる
former	前者
physiological illusion	生理的錯覚
latter	後者
cognitive illusion	認知的錯覚
interact	相互に作用する、交流する、関係を持つ　▶ the brain's past experience of interacting with the world「外界とやり取りした脳の過去の経験」
unconscious	無意識の、無意識的
inference	推論
combine	…を結合する、混合する
common	ありふれた、日常の
reflection	鏡に映った像
skull	頭がい骨
similar	似ている、同様の
form	…を形成する
torso	胴体
fraternal twins	二卵性双生児
identical twins	一卵性双生児
sundial	日時計

Unit 10

architecture	建築
elementary school	小学校
murmur	ざわめく、つぶやく
main traffic artery	交通上の動脈、幹線道路
reduce	…を減らす、減じる
sufficiently	十分に
apart from ...	…から離れて
effective	効果的な
strategy	戦略
minimize	…を最小限にする

nuisance	妨害、迷惑行為	artificial intelligence	人工知能、AI
suburban	郊外の	danger inherent in ...	…に付いて回る危険、つきまとう危険
undeveloped	未開発の	nuclear weapon	核兵器
clear	…を取り除く、(木を)伐採する	visionary	洞察力のある人、先見の明のある人
destructive	破壊的な、有害な	life imitates art.	「人生が芸術を模倣する」という芸術を中心に考える芸術至上主義の考え方 ※英国の作家Oscar Wilde(1854-1900)の言葉から取ったもの。古代ギリシャ哲学者アリストテレスに代表される "Art imitates Life"(芸術が人生を模倣する)という考えに反するものとされる
worthwhile	価値のある、無駄ではない		
observation	観察		
damage	…に損害を与える		
busy	忙しい、混んでいる、通行量が多い		
concern	心配、懸念事項		
block	妨げる、遮断する		
compatibility	適合性、融和性		
withstand	…に耐える、抵抗する	intentionally	意図的に
solid	頑丈な	collaborate	共同で取り組む
criminal	犯罪者	inspire	…の意欲をかき立てる、…を刺激する
lit	lightの過去分詞形：(照明)…を点ける、明るくする、照らす ▶ keep well lit「十分に明るくしておく」	endeavor	努力
		reasonable	合理的な、妥当な
		vital	致命的な、極めて重要な
		deprived	貧しい
at all times	いつも、常に	job opening	仕事の空き、求人
airborne pollutants	大気汚染物質	pharmaceutical	薬剤
screen out ...	…を防ぐ、を守る	from a distance	遠くから
buzz	ブンブンうなる	Devonian period	デボン紀
mosquito	蚊	jawed fish	顎口上綱（Gnathostomata）※顎を持つ脊椎動物の分類群名
camper	キャンプをする人		
evaporate	蒸発する	placoderm	板皮類 ※古生代デボン紀に繁栄した原始的な魚類の一群
boiling point	沸点		
Unit 11		spiny shark	棘魚類（Acanthodii）※古生代シルル紀〜ペルム紀に繁栄した原始的な魚類の一群
tablet computer	(iPadなどの)タブレット型コンピュータ		
advanced technology	先端技術	igneous rock	火成岩
laptop computer	ノート型パソコン	**Unit 12**	
clue	手掛かり ▶ have no clue「わからない」	universe	宇宙
		in considerable detail	かなり詳細に
co-written	共著の ※2人以上が共同で書物を著すこと	Jupiter	木星
		Saturn	土星
besides	…以外に、に加えて	Hubble image	ハッブル望遠鏡画像
genius	天才、才能	planet	惑星
cinematography	映画撮影術	abstract	抽象的な
camera angle	カメラアングル ※写真を撮る際の被写体に対するカメラの角度・配置	element	元素、成分
		disoriented	方向がわからなくなっている
perspective	物の見方、観点	goldfish	金魚
impact	影響、影響力	tank	水槽

speck	ちり、微塵
unimaginably	想像を絶するほど

Unit 13

straighten	…をまっすぐにする、整える
solar system	太陽系
Proxima Centauri	プロキシマ・ケンタウリ ※1915年に発見された太陽系から最も近い恒星、4.2光年離れたケンタウルス座の中にある赤色矮星
Alpha Centauri	ケンタウルス座α星系 ※ケンタウルス座の1等星
southern hemisphere	南半球
Sirius	シリウス ※おおいぬ座の1等星
Space Shuttle	スペースシャトル、宇宙連絡船
definitely	確かに、もちろん

Unit 14

Local Arm of the Milky Way Galaxy	天の川銀河のオリオン腕 ※天の川銀河系の中心から伸びる複数の「腕（スパイラル・アーム）」の形状部分
Galactic Bulge	銀河系のバルジ、銀河の中心にある膨らみ
Galactic Center	銀河系の中心
massive	巨大な
black hole	ブラックホール ※高密度・大質量で強い重力のため、光や熱を放出するエネルギーを使い果たして崩壊した天体
density	密度
revolution	回転
Large Magellanic Cloud	大マゼラン雲
Small Magellanic Cloud	小マゼラン雲
Local Group	局部銀河群 ※天の川銀河も所属する銀河群
Andromeda Galaxy	アンドロメダ銀河
Virgo Supercluster	おとめ座超銀河団（局部超銀河団） ※銀河系（天の川銀河）、アンドロメダ銀河、大マゼラン雲などが形成する局部銀河群を含む超銀河団
Laniakea Supercluster	ラニアケア超銀河団 ※2014年新たに提唱された超銀河団で、天の川銀河が属する局部銀河群やおとめ座超銀河団を含む